# The Bugle Sounded One Note

## Denys Stephen Heward

To Tony

I want to thank you for your most generous financial support of my 'Book for Bursaries Project'! Now I can truly forgive you for asking Sally Johnson to the LCC Grad Dance before I did. I am so indebted to you and the Class of '63 for your over-whelming support. It is a bond of friendship that I will always treasure. I hope my book rekindles some happy memories. Live your passions and inspire others!

Denys

Library and Archives Canada Cataloguing in Publication

Heward, Denys Stephen, 1946-
   The bugle sounded one note / Denys Stephen Heward.

ISBN 978-1-897336-44-1

   1. Heward, Denys Stephen, 1946-. 2. Lower Canada College – Faculty –
Biography. 3. Teachers – Québec (Province) – Montréal – Biography.
4. Montréal (Québec) – Biography. I. Title.

LA2325.H475A3 2009             371.10092             C2009-904203-7

Foreword and author bio by Paul A. Keyton,
   A.Victor Badian and Jane Martin

Inside design by Studio Melrose/Ted Sancton

Printed in Canada

Price-Patterson Ltd.
Canadian Publishers, Montreal, Quebec, Canada
www.pricepatterson.com

ISBN 1897336-446

## Special Thanks

I am grateful and indebted to my peers from the Classes of '63 and '64, and to family and friends, who rallied in an overwhelming manner to support my "Book for Bursaries Project," and whose sponsorship has made possible the publication of *The Bugle Sounded One Note*.

I would like to extend a special thank you to I.E.M. Griffiths, my great friend and LCC's long-time Senior Art teacher, for creating such a strikingly unique design for the front cover of this book.

Thank you for purchasing my book and in so doing supporting bursaries at Lower Canada College. As the cost of an LCC education keeps rising, I feel that it is imperative that more bursaries be made available to assist deserving students who might otherwise not be able to attend. If you enjoy my story and would like to further support the Denys Heward Book for Bursaries Fund, please contact the LCC Advancement office at advancement@lcc.ca. Your donation would be greatly appreciated.

# Foreword

Everyone has heard the phrase, "it changed the course of history." That is what one of Montreal and Canada's most prestigious private schools, Lower Canada College, has accomplished for so many of its alumni – including a young Denys Heward.

Denys was a student at LCC from 1955 to 1965, the beginning of a long relationship with the institution. While his school days were not easy due to significant learning difficulties, his unique, often maverick, ways of dealing with the system make for hilarious reading. His dogged perseverance and emerging passion for history would see him graduate and head off to university. Upon graduation, Denys was invited back to his alma mater to stand on the other side of the desk and experience life as a teacher.

During his 35 years in the classroom, Denys' abiding determination was that learning should be "fun" and that a student's time at school should be the best time of his or her day. He recognized that teaching must adapt to individual students' needs, and that "learning is a lifelong journey that is driven by passion." Denys' natural ability to connect with students and his ingenious methods for galvanizing their interest found their focus in his approach to teaching history. His annual "History Night" evenings established an LCC tradition that continues to this day.

Everyone who knew Denys as a fellow student or colleague, or had him as a teacher, will appreciate this insightful memoir. Through many anecdotes and musings about his days on Royal Avenue – often humorous and sometimes touching – Denys recollects how his life was changed for the better due to his relationship with the School.

It is said that teachers are born, not made, and Denys was an outstanding teacher who always strove to educate and inspire his many students in the true LCC spirit of *Non Nobis Solum* – Not for Ourselves Alone.

In loving memory of
Anne Heward Legein and Richard A. Barrett,
two outstanding teachers, who, regrettably,
were taken from us in the prime of their lives.

And for Michael Farhat '05,
whose life truly exemplified
*Non Nobis Solum.*

# Contents

## Introduction
# The Odds Were Against Me

In 1976, a unique event occurred during my grade five Canadian history course that aptly encapsulates my teaching career. Count Frontenac was being recalled from New France to France, and I really wanted my students to remember this event. In our old classrooms, the rooms were lit by a series of fluorescent lighting units that were approximately four feet long and a foot in width. Suspended from the ceiling by four, three-foot metal poles, they were basically indestructible.

On the day in question, I put my chair on top of my teacher's desk, climbed onto the chair and then onto the lighting fixture. Poised on top of one of the lights, representing the cliffs at Quebec, I intended to leap across the Atlantic to France by jumping down from my perch. There I was staring down at my students, my histrionics holding their undivided attention. Then it happened. No, the bars holding the lighting fixture did not give way, but rather, following a knock on my classroom door in walked Mr. Paul Keyton, the Director of the Junior School, with two prospective parents.

I must give my students credit, for they didn't react out of the ordinary, but instead stood up out of politeness, acting as if it were perfectly normal for Mr. Heward to be, quite literally, hanging from the ceiling. From my unconventional teaching post, I smiled sheepishly and gave an abashed wave. Mr. Keyton did not stay long, and he left my classroom door open when he exited. From out in the hallway, I could hear him say, "That's Mr. Heward's classroom. He has very unorthodox methods, but he gets the job done."

At recess time, I rushed to his office to apologize and tried to explain.

"Please Paul! Next time, tell me when you are coming around on a tour with prospective parents, and I promise you I won't be up in the lights."

"Don't do anything differently," Paul said. "Just do what you always do. I know you do strange things in your classroom, but your students love them and they work."

Of course, my story does not start with my career as a teacher. To begin at the beginning, we need to move to the other side of the desk and back to my trials and tribulations as an elementary school student in the 1950's.

One day in grade three at Roslyn School in Westmount, my adored teacher took away my fountain pen because my penmanship was so bad, leaving me to be the only student in a class of thirty-five who had to use a pencil. I was so humiliated that I proclaimed, "If you are taking my pen away, you might as well have my ink." In those days, school desks were outfitted with a hole bored into the upper right corner, which perfectly held a bottle of liquid ink. In my frustration, I picked up the bottle, which happened to be uncapped, and tossed it to her. With blue ink flowing down the front of her dress, she said not a word, but bent down, took me by the hand and out of the classroom. She brought me along the corridor, down a set of stairs to the main floor to the east end of the building, and deposited me in the all-girls' class.

There I spent the next five days, and the best week of my early school life. I knew most of the girls and was quickly adopted as the class pet. Unfortunately, it was not to last. A week later the principal, Mr. Penrose, came in to the class and asked me what I was doing there. Without divulging the reason why, I told him that my teacher had brought me here. He paused for a second, and then told me to go back to my homeroom. Back up the stairs and along the corridor I went, and knocked on the door of my old classroom. My teacher looked at me with a stern face, but didn't say a word as I returned to my seat. However she never again took away my pen!

This was only one of many school-related situations that peppered my primary school years. The odds were against me: not only was I a converted leftie, but was also afflicted with Attention Deficit Hyperactivity Disorder (ADHD) and dyslexia. I did things differently, and had major difficulties with reading and writing – how could a student with these difficulties succeed? In my youth, schools were a world of fountain pens and precise penmanship; teachers did not appreciate the left-handed student, whose hand would almost invariably sweep over the fresh ink, not allowing it to dry before becoming a messy splotch. Naturally left-handed children were often forced, as I was, to write with their right hand. There was little awareness of learning problems or resources for teachers in the early 1950's. Children who were "different" had to learn to adjust according to the norms.

I survived three years at Roslyn School, but by the end of grade three I could barely read or write, and my parents were becoming increasingly anxious. They longed to provide me with the best possible education, and wanted me to attend a school such as Lower Canada College. They had heard of Mrs. Eileen Hodgson, who taught grade four (then called Form Upper Two), and who was known to have achieved miracles with students such as myself. Another factor that had to be taken into consideration was the impending implementation of entrance examinations at LCC in the coming year. As I was barely literate, my parents reasoned that I needed to be enrolled now, or I would lose my chance. It would seem that my parents were smarter than I realized, as they had the wisdom to recognize that in order to succeed I would need every possible educational advantage and LCC had a staff of truly dedicated teachers. My parents had no doubt whatsoever as to where I should go. Little did they know how long a relationship I would have with the School.

# Chapter One
# The Walk Up Royal Avenue

In his book *Non Nobis Solum*, former Headmaster D.S. Penton describes the early days of LCC when boys and staff alike alighted from the streetcar on Sherbrooke Street and walked up Royal Avenue to the School (Penton, 49). In September of 1955, I joined the ranks of generations of LCC students who would make this trek up to the hallowed doors and the life-enriching education that lay beyond.

I remember walking slowly up Royal Avenue from Notre-Dame-de-Grâce Avenue to attend my first day of classes. In those days, NDG Avenue was a two-way street and the No. 104 bus stopped right at the corner. We rode on buses now seen only in old movies; large heavy machines made of brown metal and held together with a mass of rivets. These were especially prominent on the eyebrow-like parts of the bus above the front windows, which sloped inward at about a seventy-five degree angle. With engines that roared like angry wild animals, these buses were almost indestructible, but they had lots of seats and carried many a student to and from school each day.

The junior boys had to wear "breeches", woollen leggings that were itchy and uncomfortable and very, very English. It must be noted that LCC under its founder, Dr. Charles Fosbery, had all the trappings of a 19th century English grammar school. Built in 1909, the physical plant was not very imposing, simply a rather large two-storey rectangular building of weathered dark brick. There was a heavy green door at the south end, which was the Junior School entrance, while the senior boys disappeared down two sets of stairs that wound their way down the sides of and underneath the main entrance. Those boys lucky enough to ride their bicycles to school stored them in a long shed covered with sheets of tin behind the building, reminiscent of a British air-raid shelter from the Second World War.

Entering LCC for the first time, I noticed how worn the stone step outside the door was, indented from decades of young feet entering and leaving the School. The entrance led into the basement, which was sub-divided into several sections. The Junior School locker room was a drab grey room crammed with tall metal lockers. On the terrazzo floor the sporting equipment was housed in large wire mesh cages. With the high ceilings exposing a network of pipes, the whole basement scene could be politely described as neo-Industrial Revolution.

While not pretty, it served a purpose, and the morning assemblies for both the Junior and Senior Schools were held down there, with students lined up in long files by grade. The grade twelve Prefects were in charge of the Senior School assembly, presided over by Headmaster Dr. Stephen Penton. The Junior School teachers ran the assembly for the younger boys. They were assisted by monitors from grade six in my first year, and then from grade seven thereafter, as it was moved down to the Junior School after Mr. Geoffrey Merrill's first year as Junior School Director. It struck me that the basement area was designed for maximum utility at the minimum cost. However, the design of the Junior School locker room served us well (especially during the winter), providing a platform for us to flip gum cards against the walls where the terrazzo floor curved upwards to form a base for each boy's locker. Many a hockey and baseball collection was won by nimble throwing. Oh, to have those valuable collections today!

### Scents ....Smells ....Enticing Odours

There were many types of smells that emanated from the basement. The boys' washroom, unchanged for decades and with little air circulation, had a very distinctive odour that was created by the trapped moisture of the shower facilities, making the already stagnant air extremely dense. This was combined with a strong undercurrent of smells ranging from stale milk cartons and much used drain-cleaning fluids, not to mention the reek of body odour emanating from sporting equipment, the boys' lockers and sometimes the boys themselves! There was the resinous scent of Dustbane, used nightly to clean the terrazzo floors, and in the winter season the smell of pine tar drifted from the cross-country skis, which were continuously being tuned for upcoming ski races. Mixed in with this was the reek of formaldehyde from the biology lab, where dead rats and other specimens were kept for dissection.

But while there was many a stink, there were also aromas to be savoured, such as the Tuck Shop's bewitching aroma of sugar-coated raisin buns, and the preparation of meals from the cafeteria. The scents drifting forth from the School's expansive kitchen permeated through the basement, and if the windows were open and the wind was just right, they would creep up to the main floor as well. The enticing smells of roast beef or the Chef's famous spaghetti sauce made it hard for me to concentrate during that last period before descending to the Dining Room.

On the main floor was the Banda machine, an early form of copier, which contributed to the sensory melee, with constant whiffs of alcohol that drifted down the long corridors. While most of us hated the class tests, we certainly loved to sniff the freshly printed test pages! It was especially rewarding if the teacher had just run off the copies a few minutes prior to the class. The other familiar smell was tobacco; almost every teacher smoked, and several teachers used a pungent pipe tobacco. The staffroom was usually engulfed in a cloud of smoke, and the teachers' clothing carried that sweet smell of tobacco into the classrooms, whether they were smokers or not. There was also that stale odour of tobacco breath, which you had to endure if you were unfortunate enough to require a teacher's individual attention at your desk. What a contrast to today! Forgive me, for while I have digressed into these observations a half a century after the fact, it is amazing how tenacious the staying power is of smells in one's memory – and how specific odours can invoke images that are long since past.

I began my relationship with LCC as a very young boy. My first day was made even more special by one of my new classmates, Charles Douglas, the resident class genius. At recess time on that first day, he presented me with a copy of the School song that he had taken the trouble to write out on my behalf. So "*Non Nobis Solum*" (not for ourselves alone) was presented to me an hour after I arrived on Royal Avenue. Due to the diligent efforts of Mrs. Eileen Hodgson (bless her heart!), who worked like a Trojan, I was nearly able to function by the end of grade four. I will never forget her love, kindness and encouragement. While my overall average would remain near the bottom of the class ranks for several years, I was quickly developing a steadfast attachment to life at LCC.

### "Ya! Mister Kie'fer!"

One of my favourite moments as a student occurred in grade six. We had a young teacher, Mr. Jim Keith, who taught us history. While he was a really likeable, decent guy (who later in his life would become Chancellor

of Mount Allison University), he repeatedly made one grievous faux pas.
In our class there was a new student named Tim Hayman, a talented athlete
who became one of the guys very quickly. It was amazing how fast a new
student who was a good athlete was accepted. What most of us didn't know
was that Tim had transferred from the French school system, and he was
very anxious and self-conscious. Mr. Keith fuelled this anxiety by mis-
takenly and repeatedly calling Hayman – Hyman. Tim gently but regularly
pointed out that his name was Hayman, not Hyman, and would he please
call him as such?

Unfortunately, in our next history class, Mr. Keith did it again. At this
point Tim was at the end of his rope and, staunch Roman Catholic that he
was, answered Mr. Keith in his best Yiddish accent, arms out-stretched
with his palms and fingers pointed upward. "Ya Mister Kie'fer! Vat do you
Vant?" We all sat dumbfounded. Mr. Keith didn't know what to say … but
he never called Tim 'Hyman' again! Of course, in the late 1950's people
paid little attention to the niceties of political correctness. They simply
said what was on their minds. I recently saw Tim at a Vancouver LCC
Reunion and we shared a laugh about that unforgettable day. It's amazing
how a random classroom blooper can sometimes stick with you forever.

Forty-two years later, Tim proved that he can still bring a smile to my
face when we reminisced about another incident. In the summer of 1972,
several years after graduation, Tim had returned to Montreal for a visit, and
went to the bank to withdraw some money. There were no automatic
tellers in those days, so he was one in a long line of customers waiting
somewhat impatiently at the Royal Bank on Sherbrooke at Hampton. For
many years, this branch was the bank for the School and many LCC staff.
While still in line, Tim spotted Mr. Paul Howard, our former Latin teacher
(and all around wonderful person), sauntering his way out towards the
door. Tim called out, "Mr. Howard," who in turn replied, "Timmy
Hayman". Tim asked him, "After all the many students you have taught,
how did you ever recognize me?" Mr. Howard replied, "Oh that's easy. I
could never forget you. You were one of the worst students in Latin that I
ever taught!" Of course Mr. Howard, who was slightly hard of hearing at
the time, said it in a loud enough voice so that everyone in the long queue
heard the remark.

### The Sugar Fix

The lower grades did not have access to the Tuck Shop during the morning recess, and since milk was not provided at lunch, small milk cartons were delivered in a long rectangular wooden box directly to the Junior School classrooms. It was a great idea, but these containers of milk were often processed an hour or two earlier by the ladies of the kitchen staff, and this meant that the milk was usually warm and not the refreshing treat that it should have been. In the higher grades, we were issued Tuck Cards, which we used to collect our milk from Mrs. Margaret Jones, the wife of Mr. Jack Jones, the School's live-in Maintenance Supervisor. Mrs. Jones was a wonderful Scottish lady who tried to appear gruff and tough, but who in reality was a very endearing individual. They had a small apartment on the top floor where the Advancement Office and the upstairs photocopy room are today.

What I remember most about Mrs. Jones, apart from her heavy Scottish accent that we all mimicked, is that she would let you trade in your milk coupon with a small payment of two cents for a delicious sticky-bun coated with icing sugar and filled with raisins. Our daily treats at the Tuck Shop may not sound like much to modern-day LCC students, but we did not have access to nutritious snacks, second helpings at lunch, an unlimited salad and sandwich bar, plus an abundance of vending machines. It's no wonder that I was always hungry!

### Lions in Winter

While Mrs. Jones was for the most part a kind individual, she was a force to be reckoned with if you crossed her. This became apparent nearly two decades later when Victor Badian, my closest friend on the LCC Staff, was a young master making his way up to school one winter morning. He was driving up Royal Avenue in a snow-and-ice storm in the two tire tracks that were available to him and, as most parents and LCC Staff know, that little slope on Royal just above NDG Avenue is treacherous in wintry weather. If you are forced to slow down or your car loses momentum, your vehicle will undoubtedly become stuck and thus create a traffic jam.

That morning, Vic turned the corner and gunned his car, wheels spinning on the ice but still gaining forward momentum. Ah! But there was Mrs. Jones, walking as best she could in one of the tire tracks and carrying several large packages. Normally the consummate gentleman, Vic in this case did not dare to stop; he simply honked his horn and kept on coming. Poor Mrs. Jones was forced to leap into the snow bank to save herself from Vic's oncoming vehicle! From that day forward, and no matter how often he apologized, his bun was virtually thrown at him at the Tuck Shop. The silver lining to this mishap routinely occurred in the staffroom, where Vic would re-enact for any and all to see his rendition of Mrs. Jones throwing a sugar bun at him. As Vic has an insatiable sweet tooth, this performance was delivered on a fairly regular basis. Many years after the Joneses had retired from LCC, I paid a visit to Mrs. Jones while she was convalescing at the Catherine Booth Hospital. She hadn't changed a bit, and a warm smile spread across her face as we talked about the old days. What a character she was!

### *"Jocks vs. Education"*

In the late 1960's, under the tenure of LCC's fourth Headmaster Mr. Geoffrey Merrill, there was a saying: "Send your son to LCC if he is a jock and to Selwyn House if you want a good education." There may have been elements of truth in that statement, but the majority of us were very content with our daily existence. Life at a school without athletics was unimaginable to the average LCC boy. The school was well kitted out for the active boy: It had its own artificial ice rink which opened on March 30th, 1955, and across from the main building was a massive playing field large enough for nearly three football or soccer fields, several softball diamonds and even a cricket pitch until 1991. It was only natural that sports and games became an every-day activity.

Ironically, the current Headmaster Chris Shannon attended and graduated from Selwyn House School. His absence from LCC during his high school years can be excused, as he attended LCC for grade twelve where he was a pivotal player on the Senior Lions hockey team and added his considerable expertise to football and rugby. Of his days as a student at LCC he has fond memories:

> "My introduction to LCC was at the pre-season football
> training camp. We were coached by the legendary Dave
> Wood, who had effectively made his full team before the

season. So making the starting roaster was a challenge, but something I managed to do with a little persistence. In fact, that team had an outstanding year – undefeated until the city championship, when we lost in a close match. Overall, my one-year experience in Grade 12 was most enjoyable. I thoroughly enjoyed English with Dave Morton, Geography with Doug MacLean and calculus with Tom Wright. I had played a fair amount of rugby before coming to LCC and Tom Wright was very keen to have myself and a couple of other ex-Selwyn students bring some experience to his squad. It was under the persistent guidance of Mr. Wright that the LCC Senior Rugby team won its first city championship in the spring of 1976 at a match played at the old Autostade where the Alouettes then played. We were the warm-up match to Quebec vs. the British Lion All Stars. It was fun to defeat some of my old pals from Selwyn in that game. As is one of its trademarks today, LCC was indeed a welcoming school where involvement and commitment usually led to success."

Not only did many of us almost live on the LCC fields in the fall and spring, but we had countless games of ball hockey in the open area where the math classrooms and the science labs now stand. There was no science wing at all until 1959, and even then it was, as described by D.S Penton, "a semi-basement building with an entrance from the north end of the Dining Room." The building was constructed so that two more storeys could be added in the future" (Penton, 237). Until then, that large flat area was ideal for ball hockey and when we lost that space, the school set up two ball hockey rinks on the field where the Webster Learning Activity Center now stands.

Our chief competitor was Selwyn House School, and they did not have access to such facilities as an artificial rink or our magnificent playing fields. In part because of this, our real rival in sports was not Selwyn, but Loyola High School. If you lost to Loyola, you were expected to hang your head in shame for a long period of penitence. It was funny, losing to another school was not such a big deal, but a loss to the boys from Loyola was a very different indeed. Of course, it is more than likely that the boys at Loyola felt the same way about us, and this led to an outstanding rivalry. Over the years, many a City Championship came down to a battle between LCC and Loyola. My sympathy goes out to a few of the Loyola boys, such as John Corker and the Barakett brothers, who came over to LCC for grade twelve and had to face (and best!) their former team-mates in football and hockey.

### Two Coaching Legends

The intense rivalry between LCC and Loyola was also fuelled by the fact that both schools had two of the finest high school football and hockey coaches in the city, Dave Wood (LCC) and Ed Meagher (Loyola). The large number of Senior Football and Hockey Championships won by both schools during the 1950's and 60's is a testimony to these two outstanding individuals. It was commonly acknowledged that Dave Wood was the (slightly) better football coach, while Ed Meagher got the nod for hockey. If you have ever had the privilege of playing for either of these exemplary gentlemen, you know what I mean – quite simply, you were coached by the best. Dave was a very quiet coach. While he was a man of few words, what he had to say spoke volumes, and there are some statements that I will never forget. If his team had won the championship the year before, he had this to say to his players:

"Now if you were on this team last year, you are a champion. If you are replacing someone from last year's team, then you have to play like a champion."

"Only your very best effort is acceptable."

"The first game of the season is the second most important game, the last game, the Championship game is the most important."

"I want you to hit the opposing players as hard as you possibly can, just be sure it is a clean hit."

I had the honour of having Dave Wood as my coach, but I knew Ed Meagher only by reputation. In the 1980's, I coached the Senior Hockey Lions with Allen Wightman and we were invited annually to play in the Loyola Hockey Tournament. In my student days, I had the good fortune of playing on the LCC Senior Hockey Championship teams in 1963 and 64. At my first Loyola Tournament reception, following the Friday evening games, I spotted Ed Meagher. Wishing to introduce myself, I went over to speak with him.

"Hi! Mr. Meagher," I said, "I just wanted to meet you as I have heard so much about you over the years. In fact, I played against your hockey teams in 1963 and 64."

Ed Meagher looked at me:

"What is your name?"

"Denys Heward," I replied.

He smiled and said,

"Oh! Yes! You were the goalie for LCC in those years."

I was astonished. During my thirty-five years at LCC I coached a variety of sports teams, and while I remember a few athletes very well, I do not recall all of them. Here was a man who, nearly twenty years after the fact, could remember a player and his position from an opposing team. We soon became friends and I looked forward to greeting Ed each year at the Loyola Tournament that now honours his name.

### Fear and Discipline

Games and sports were built into our weekly schedules and every boy participated. However, a determined classroom performance was also expected. LCC had strict discipline, and the stick was used as a quick and efficient means of maintaining order. We all knew the limits of what we were permitted to do, so if we were caned, it was usually because we had knowingly broken the rules. As a student, I received this punishment for a wide assortment of misdemeanours. On one occasion I made the mistake of telling my father, who then proceeded to give me double treatment at home with orders to report any future 'whackings'. Needless to say, I never again made any reference to my misdeeds at school.

There was only one teacher whom I feared during my years as a student. He was a big, strong man with a booming voice who had a reputation for having a bad temper on occasion. The irony is that he was one of the few teachers who never whacked me. He was my first boss when I joined the staff as a teacher and over the years, became a close friend and mentor. With a heart of gold, he was one of the most caring, compassionate people I encountered during my time at LCC.

The teacher in question was Mr. Dave Wood, and we first encountered each other when I was in grade seven. I remember one time sitting in Mr.

Merrill's 7A class during the first period after the lunch break – in a class-room adjacent to Mr. Wood's. Our respective blackboards were separated only by a wall, so that any serious vibrations in one classroom could be felt in the other one. On that particular day, it appeared that 7B was having a bit of a 'pressure period' – dust kept emanating from the cracks between the slate blackboards – as Mr. Wood was obviously a little upset at something or someone. Suddenly, a chill ran down my spine as I thought, *Oh! My God!* Didn't we have Mr. Wood next period for grammar? And, *Oh! No!* I had forgotten to do a rather large grammar assignment. For all my misdemeanours, I seldom forgot to do my homework. It had just been an oversight but, in the mood that Mr. Wood was in, I knew that I was in for it. There was no escaping this unfortunate situation – or was there? My mind raced; I had to do something, or else! In those days, students rarely challenged their teachers in the classroom, but I would have to chance it.

The bell signalled the change in periods, and a few moments later in stormed Mr. Wood. Slamming his load of books onto the teacher's desk, he turned to the class and snarled, "No! I am not in a good mood!" My moment of truth had come. I rose smartly to my feet and called out in front of the stunned classroom:

"Mr. Wood! Sir!" I stated firmly, "Mr. Wood, there has been a discussion in this classroom. Many of the boys have said that you are unfair, Sir, that you would 'whack' a boy even if he hadn't done anything." I paused ever so briefly. "But Mr. Wood! I want you to know that I came to your defence. I said that you were a very fair man and that you would never 'whack' a boy if he hadn't done anything!"

"Of course I wouldn't 'whack' a boy if he hadn't done anything," blurted out Mr. Wood.

"Sir," I continued, rather sheepishly, "I didn't do my homework."

Mr. Wood was somewhat taken aback … but when he recovered he smiled and gave me until the next day to complete the assignment. That was the beginning of my lifelong relationship with this outstanding man and teacher. Not only was he my teacher and my coach, but at the time I joined the staff he was the Director of the Junior School. I have worked very closely with him for many years, both as a student and a peer.

There was only one time that I took a caning with a smile on my face.

In grade nine I had a certain English teacher (who shall remain nameless) who may have known his stuff but was not able to communicate with his students. He was not well-liked and was often painted in an ugly light by his students. On the afternoon in question, I was doing much too much talking while he was teaching. He stopped his lecture, glared at me over his heavy, horn-rimmed glasses and said, "If you think that you can teach this class better than I can, Heward, then come up here and teach it!" I needed no further invitation: I grabbed my poetry book, marched up to the front of the class and started to teach. I was rightfully kicked out of the class and punished for my impertinence, but it was worth it.

### The Morning Ritual

Most of the students from my era would arrive to school early, usually around 7:30 a.m. We would immediately deposit our book bags at our lockers and head out to the field for a pick-up game of touch football. Starting out with only a handful of players, gradually the teams would grow larger and larger as late-comers arrived and joined us on the field. We would play until the last possible minute before school started at 8:30 a.m. Our early morning football games were considered wonderful by us, but not to our poor mothers. As we always played in our school uniforms, they had to contend with the many rips and tears, not to mention those stubborn grass stains. Sometimes we disposed of our oxfords (as we could run faster in our socks), and would often also discard our blue blazers, leaving them to be crushed under foot.

At recess, lunchtime and after school, it was usually more of the same. While we were supposedly playing "touch" football our games were often quite rough and ready, something akin to rugby. While I and my classmates may have missed out, in 1971 the beginnings of a rugby program were put into motion. Under the inspiration and leadership of mathematics teacher Tom Wright, an incomparable Irishman, whose true passion in life was rugby, the game began to take hold at LCC. Today his legacy is carried on, as rugby is now one of the school's most popular sports, loved by the girls as much as the boys – if not more so (LCC went fully coeducational in 1995). Is this a sign of the times? I think so!

### Rabbit Ears ....Daytime Baseball ....Sheer Terror

The LCC students of my day didn't have cell phones and other technological gadgets such as BlackBerrys, iPods and MP3 Players. Heck, we didn't even have girls to captivate our attention! Television was only just beginning (in black and white of course); stations broadcasted during very limited hours and cable was as of yet unheard of. I can still remember that in the mid 1950's Montreal's CBMT Channel 6, in its earliest stages, only had programming running from 4:00 to 9:00 p.m. We had to use "rabbit ears" in order to get reception – an aerial which consisted of two extendable metal antennae, which projected upwards at strange angles from their large plastic bulb-like base. These antennae had to be adjusted regularly in order to get a clear image, and oftentimes some steel wool affixed to the top of each rod would make a significant difference in reducing the "snow" (static). The other alternative was to have a family member, friend or colleague actually place his or her hand on the aerial, which would immensely improve the reception; that is, it would improve reception for everyone but the person holding the antennae.

By the 1960's television had become more affordable, and it was quickly adopted as the preferred medium of the general public. The World Series games were played in the afternoon (as night baseball games were still a thing of the future) but if we were lucky, a kind teacher would let us bring a radio to the classroom. Many of us had those small transistor radios, some equipped with an ear plug.

Fortunately, one of my classmates (and good friend) Bruce Jenkins lived just down the street from school, at the corner of NDG and Royal Avenue. So during our lunch hour we could sneak down to his house and catch a few innings of those memorable games – so long as we didn't get caught leaving school grounds! I usually got my innings in, with the exception on one occasion when I got nabbed returning for afternoon classes. But what was a week's detention compared to seeing three innings of Sandy Koufax and the Dodgers mowing down those damned Yankees? The year 1963 was a great one for baseball, with the Dodgers winning the World Series. Since the Montreal Royals had always been a Dodger farm team, I was a diehard Dodger fan until the arrival of the Expos in 1969.

World series aside, LCC did more than just promote athletics from 1955 to 1965. Stephen Penton, the school's third Headmaster (1941-1968), valued diversity and sought to encourage open-mindedness and dignity. He was a great supporter of the School, attending almost every home game played by LCC's teams. He also encouraged teachers to promote all sorts of other non-athletic activities, such as the stamp, photography and debating clubs.

Every year the Senior School held a gymnastics display under the direction of our much loved physical training educator, Major Howard Gibb. 'Gibby', as we called him, had somehow managed to miraculously survive as a tail-gunner during World War II. Looking at the statistics, most tail-gunners didn't last many missions, making it one of the most dangerous positions in the RAF. In the Memorial Gym, and sometimes in the RMR Armoury in Westmount, each class would in turn perform for the assembled audience. The best classes did some serious gymnastic routines, while the less agile classes performed simplified choreographies using long wooden broom handles.

Many of us were active athletically. The House System, each house bearing the name of a distinguished alumnus, was very much a presence in our day-to-day lives. The four original houses, Woods, French, Russel and Drummond, would make up the teams for the intra-mural sports program which had a large role in the school's routine. The eight-man house Tackle Football League for students in grades eight, nine and ten was something many students experienced in their time at LCC, whether they wanted to or not. Only members of the football teams were exempt.

I played fullback and linebacker for French House. During one particular game I broke my big toe whilst blocking a kick-off return; I could barely walk. I would limp out onto the field and into my position as a fullback. However, as soon as I was handed the ball my adrenaline would start pumping full tilt, letting me run without a trace of my injury. At least until the play was over – then I would limp back to the huddle for the next play.

Another athletic memory is the Senior Hockey Team trip to North-wood at Lake Placid, New York, for two great matches, with the added bonus of a side trip to the Olympic bobsled run nearby. For those of you who have never had the dubious pleasure of sitting four inches off the ice while careening down a narrow icy channel at speeds in excess of 100km an hour, I can assure you that it is a toss-up between consummate joy and sheer terror! I can still feel the 'S' curves – where your internal organs seem to be plastered to one side of the run, and left there as the bobsled lurches over to the other side. At the time I thought it to be a once-in-a-lifetime experience. However, a few years ago after a day of cross-country skiing at Lake Placid, I took my son down the same course. I was happy to have had an interval of 25 years between runs!

### Dyslexia in the 60's

In my day, most teachers were not aware of dyslexia or other learning disabilities. "He is just an excitable young fellow who can't spell," they would say. As a young boy, I didn't know what was wrong with me. While I tried my best to achieve, I recognized that I was different from my peers. Despite my poor report cards, I knew that I wasn't stupid; I just couldn't express myself on paper. I remember well studying for hours in grade seven for a major spelling test. Unfortunately, my study tactics were all wrong. Standard spelling tests follow the procedure wherein the teacher will recite a word, and the student must try to record it correctly. However, I did the exact opposite, spelling out the words orally as my mother asked me them. On the test the next Monday, I got 98 out of 100 words wrong; my teacher then said that I hadn't studied very hard. Of course this was not true, as I had spent hours reviewing the words. Furthermore, he thought me to be careless, noting, "Look, you have even written your letter 'e' backwards in several places." It was truly disheartening to have worked so hard and to have scored so poorly. I didn't know that I was dyslexic and that there was a legitimate reason for my poor performance. My self-esteem suffered. I was miserable and I felt like a loser and was seriously questioning what I was going to do with my life, if I ever managed to get through school at all.

Less caring teachers at LCC simply said that I was stupid. However, while doing some research on the topic several years ago, I was surprised to learn that many students with dyslexia are often more intelligent than the average. They have it all upstairs, but something gets lost in translation when they try to put their thoughts down on paper. If it were standard protocol to allow dyslexic students to take formal examinations through oral questioning, they would score much higher. Having lived my life with this condition, I know the frustrations of not being able to spell or truly express myself with the written word. In primary school, I disliked comic books, which were all the rage at that time. Quite simply, I could not read the captions and was too embarrassed to admit it. With time, practice and often much frustration, one learns to accept, adapt, adjust and compensate for one's weaknesses.

As I grew older, I endeavoured to learn more about my condition and I discovered someone who suffered as I did in school, but who has since become enormously successful. That person is Sir Richard Branson, a British entrepreneur best known for his *Virgin* brand which is made up of over 360 companies. While his academic performance as a student was poor, he learned to adapt, adjust and compensate for his problems – he did things differently because he had to. When he was at school, his headmaster predicted he would wind up "either a millionaire or in jail" (Branson, March 2007). The fact is he did both. His maverick strategies worked for him and allowed him to amass a significant fortune. From failure to success, he was knighted in 1999 for his "services to entrepreneurship." Due to his learning difficulties, he developed a different way of looking at the world of business. In a similar fashion, I took an unorthodox approach to teaching, and without question, modifying many of the pedagogical rules and employing unconventional methodologies. Branson's struggles in school parallelled my own. I certainly felt like a kindred soul when I read that "Since nobody had ever heard of dyslexia, being unable to read, write or spell just meant to the rest of the class and teachers that you were either stupid or lazy" (Branson, March 2007).

As luck would have it, I had some great teachers who looked beyond my erratic behaviour and questionable performance in the classroom. They could see into my personality, understand my passions and perceive my potential and determination. Here was a boy who would die trying if nothing else! Learning disabilities are a lifelong struggle as they seldom disappear. You have to learn to compensate and manage them, but they are always lurking in the background, ready to cause no end of trouble. One of the great dilemmas a teacher faces is that while you can understand the academic problems your students with learning difficulties have, you really can't appreciate the frustrations they encounter on a daily basis unless you have lived with them yourself.

In my early years of schooling, I developed a sort of tape recorder mind. I could remember almost word for word what was said to me by a teacher, provided of course I was interested in the subject at hand. I especially loved trivia and could religiously recite material that I found fascinating, but unfortunately these 'factoids' were not likely to find their way on to any test. I was developing a love of learning, but only for those topics that interested me. Luckily, I was introduced at an early age to what was to become my passion in life: history. Ironically, this did not happen during my early social studies classes but rather during my introduction to Latin. Like all languages, Latin is rule-bound and I was hopeless at learning all of the intricacies of its grammar and syntax. Why would anybody in his or her right mind place the verb at the end of the sentence? On the other hand, I enjoyed the vocabulary and I loved the heroic stories of the Romans. Here were men who came to life on the printed page. They had their faults and weaknesses, but they battled adversity and became conquerors and leaders of nations. They showed what an incredible work ethic and discipline could do, and they seemed to live life to the fullest.

There are innumerable stories and examples from the Roman Empire, and one such heroic account from my elementary years sticks with me to this day. An overwhelming force of invading Barbarians was confronted by a small detachment of Roman soldiers whose responsibility it was to guard a narrow bridge which the enemy had to cross. The Barbarian chieftain was confronted by a Roman soldier who defiantly refused to surrender the bridge. To show the enemy commander his resolve and courage, he thrust his hand into a pot of burning coals. At that moment, the Barbarian leader reasoned that if the rest of the Roman army was like this soldier, he wouldn't stand a chance of victory. He turned his army around and retreated.

### Candid Antics

In the early 1960's, we had what was called a Candid Camera Day. Being the photography editor for the School Yearbook I was allowed, by special permission, to bring my camera to the classroom to shoot candid shots on more than just the designated day. I undertook this privilege with proper decorum for most teachers, with the exception of one of our French teachers. We had affectionately nicknamed him "Stache" due to his Hercule Poirot-like moustache. His uptight demeanour seemed, to a rogue like me, like a balloon which asked to be punctured regularly, a temptation I could hardly resist! Camera in hand, I would get out of my seat and move freely about the classroom, tapping "Stache" on the shoulder frequently while he was writing on the blackboard or sitting at his desk. As soon as he turned his head, I would flash my camera (which was equipped with large old fashioned bulbs) as close to his face as I could. I fired dozens of such shots of him all week long, but had purposely not loaded my camera with any film – I was just being as big a nuisance as I could be and loving every minute of it.

The following week, I had to ask him for one more picture (an *actual* photo this time). He replied with his usual turn of phrase, "Now, look Heward! You took hundreds of photos of me last week." Of course, I was then forced to tell him the truth that my camera had not been loaded with film! Fortunately he cooperated, and I actually took a good photo of him that day.

Many years later, when I was a relatively new member of Staff, I came across "Stache" doing some tutoring with a student in one of the upstairs classrooms. I waited until he had finished and went in to apologize for being such an atrocious nuisance when I was in his class. He smiled in his typical manner and said, "That's all right, Heward, you were really a good boy on the whole." While nothing could have been further from the truth, bless his heart, he still forgave me. I pulled a lot of 'boyish' pranks during my ten years as a student, but he was the only teacher that, later in life, I felt guilty for what I had done to him. He was a decent, caring and wonderful man who truly wanted to teach us French, but I was having too much fun (and lacked the maturity) to settle down and let him do so. He may have reached me but he didn't manage to teach me much French. It was my great loss!

*I was a skinny kid*

*In Gr. 5, with teacher Tom Gartshore (I'm 3rd from Rt, 3rd row back), 1957*

*In nets against St. Thomas, 1964*

*Dining Room in 1950's*

*Cadet inspection day, Signal Corps, 1956*

*Early 70's, when sideburns were in*

*Headmaster Geoffrey Merrill*

*My Gr 5B class in 1974*

*Lunchtime ball hockey, 1977*

*Alumni team champions, 1973*

*Typical Jr. School classroom, early 70's*

*HMS Pinafore 1976 (Merrill, Heward, T. Cobbett '76)*

*Treasure Island, 1981*

*The timekeeper - Jr. School track and field day, 1970's*

*With Kelly and Stephen, ca 1985*

# Chapter Two
# Moving On, Moving Up

In the 1960's the Junior School finished at grade seven, and grades eight through eleven made up the Senior School. On top of that was grade twelve or the Senior Academic Year, which in the current era is now known as the Pre-University Year. This transition from Junior to Senior School meant that starting in grade eight you no longer had the warmth and security of a homeroom teacher, who taught the majority of your courses and followed your everyday existence. Instead, the Senior School had a Form Master, who was responsible for overseeing your report cards and was there when needed as your advisor.

There was definitely a monitoring and support system in place, but for the first time in your academic life you were expected to stand on your own two feet. The cracks were wider and you could easily fall through them. Your teachers were for the most part subject teachers; however students would really get to know them during the many games periods or when they performed their duties as coaches of the various school teams. While I had the right attitude and was willing to try my very hardest, my reading skills were still far below par and my study skills extremely ineffective. I put in study time whenever I was not playing football or hockey, but my report cards had little to show for it. However, Wednesdays would always have a different outcome as that was Army Cadet Day.

### Dit, Dah, Dit, Dit

Every student in the Senior School automatically became a member of the LCC Cadet Corps, in affiliation with the Royal Montreal Regiment. We all had to wear the full army cadet uniform, a coarse khaki battle dress composed of pants with leg weights, jacket, perfectly shined boots, gaiters and an immaculately whitened belt. This was topped by the traditional red beret with the RMR insignia pin. I remember every September students clamouring for the highly polished pins as we collected our uniforms at the start of the year. Some students polished them so much that they had almost completely worn off the RMR crest, leaving behind nothing but a highly polished piece of brass, and the best cadets learned how to "spoon" the leather on the toe of their army boots to create a highly glossed shine. What I especially remember is that the battle dress pants did not have zippers; instead they were outfitted with the traditional six or eight buttons, which were certainly a nuisance when it came to recess and bathroom breaks!

I wore my uniform to and from school on Cadet Days, and I didn't mind that as it made me stand out on the crowded buses. Furthermore, I truly felt a sense of Canadian pride when we marched in the November 11th Remembrance Day parades. However, those long Wednesday afternoons doing marching drills on the LCC field from 3:30 to 5:00 p.m. (or later) certainly did not inspire me. Those of us who were undisciplined, poorly dressed or insubordinate had to run around the field with ancient, breech-loading World War II (or perhaps World War I) rifles held above our head. They were heavy, but sometimes the punishment broke up the monotony of the incessant marching drills. One time after one lap around the field for insubordination – a distance of about a kilometre – my lieutenant, thinking that I had learned my lesson asked me, "How did you enjoy that, Cadet Heward?" To which I replied, "Very nice, Sir! Why don't you try it yourself?" Needless to say, I was sent off again and again, as I just couldn't resist an insolent comment each time I completed a lap. It was a very tiring afternoon, but entertaining for the cadets of my platoon, several of whom had to join me for laughing at my remarks. At any rate, it was a great upper-body work out.

At LCC, there was no way to avoid the Cadet Corps. Even if there had been, my father, an ex-naval commander from World War II, thought it was great for my personal growth and a builder of discipline. I decided the next year that there had to be a better way. Fortunately there were some options within the Corps: one could join the Band, the Signal Corps or go to Army Camp in Farnham, QC during the summer and become an officer. First I decided to try the Band, but was quickly kicked out, as I couldn't play a note on the trumpet and they had more than enough drummers. Then I remembered from the year before that I had noticed that the Signal Corps was excused from the marching drills and conducted its sessions inside the school building. On top of that, Signal Corps members were dismissed around 4:15, instead of 5:00 p.m. or later like the rest of us. We would see them silently slinking down Royal Avenue as we marched around the field.

And the only marching they ever had to do was to march onto the field on Cadet Inspection Day. What a cushy job! That was definitely for me. However, the Signal Corps was serious business. Each cadet was expected to learn Morse code by sound recognition, and if you passed the test at the end of the year you earned $10, big money in those days. While I realized that I probably wasn't going to master it, I still pretended to work hard and enjoyed walking down Royal Avenue at 4:15 p.m.

I clearly remember the day of our code exam. You had to interpret a series of letters and a message and that is what we had practiced. However, our examiner from the Army reversed the order of what we had studied without telling us and keyed the messages at a very fast clip. Before I realized what was going on, I was totally lost and scored very poorly. The examiner was so frustrated with me that he sent me the letter 'L', which is dit, dah, dit, dit. He then barked at me. "What was that signal, Cadet Heward?" Instead of saying the letter, I replied, "dit, dah, dit, dit! Sir!" and thus I ingloriously failed the test.

If that wasn't bad enough, there was still Cadet Inspection Field Day to come. I was given the task of manning the switchboard for the field telephones set up all over the field. I actually enjoyed this operation, for I was situated in the shade of the great line of magnificent old poplar trees bordering the Westward Field, and then I was visited by all the girls who had come with their parents to watch. One particularly lovely young lass even brought me a cold bottle of Coca Cola. I took great pleasure in plugging and unplugging the wires and ringing up the various stations, and felt very comfortable at the controls. Naturally, we had a script to follow, and that was to be my undoing. An incoming call followed the correct dispatch, but then asked for two limousines as well. That was not in the script! "What are the limousines for," I inquired, "the big fat general?"

"I am the big fat general," barked the voice at the other end of the phone, our visiting dignitary from the Army.

"Right, away, Sir!" I replied, but it was too late. I had done it again!

Many years later, given my passion for history, I reflect back and realize that the Cadet Corps was probably a very good experience. I may not have given it my all or brought the proper attitude to it, but it did teach me the need to protect our cherished freedoms, and how societies can be organized and function to protect and better all their citizens. It certainly helped teach me to respect the sacrifices made on all our behalf by our parents as veterans, and today it gives an even deeper meaning to the current Canadian military mission in Afghanistan. We live in a volatile world, and mankind has not paid close enough attention to the lessons of history.

### Stringent Rules

Back in the classroom, my time in high school was dominated by teachers who, for the most part, practiced common views on discipline and, as individuals, were somewhat influenced by the post-war era in which they taught. Their styles and methods varied greatly; some were out of touch with their students, and yet others were very connected. However, no one could deny that they were all characters.

In some cases, there was an inability of these old-style teachers to recognize when a student was having difficulties. Certainly, several of them did not recognize, and by extension appreciate, what I was going through, as they were as stuck in their classroom practices and ways of thinking as technocrats are today. One such example of this rigidity was the situation I found myself in with Mr. Paul Howard, my grade eight Latin teacher. Mr. Howard was a teacher I really liked and was a great athlete, especially in badminton and hockey. I remember playing recreational badminton against him and feeling a great sense of accomplishment if I managed to win even a single point. He was a true gentleman and was extremely gracious and kind to me when I joined the staff, but was very rigid in the classroom. For homework, our class regularly had to translate a Latin passage into English. One day, I was called upon to translate the first paragraph of a particular passage aloud. I did so with surprising ease, but was somewhat taken aback when he asked me to continue. Mr. Howard hardly ever let anyone do more than a sentence or two, but on this particular day I was asked to translate the whole story. I did so without error and was quite pleased with myself.

When I was finished Mr. Howard, instead of congratulating me, proclaimed "Mr. Heward! You will come and see me after school for a detention." Confused, I inquired as to what I had done wrong. Mr. Howard looked at me and said, "Next time you need to translate the passage using the text. You didn't even have your book open." Usually, I would fake reading by pretending to look at the text while actually reciting from memory, but that morning I was so engrossed in the story that I had not thought to open my textbook. Being dyslexic, I had learned to adapt, adjust and compensate for my shortcomings, but some teachers could not or would not appreciate such strategies. While I didn't feel that I deserved the detention, I loved the Roman history (and still do!) to which Mr. Howard thankfully introduced me.

### Le Grand Chef

LCC had student boarders until June of 1962, when the Board of Governors decided boarding should come to an end as the bedroom space was needed to meet the needs of the ever-expanding enrolment. Boarding had very much made the School a twenty-four hour-a-day operation, even if the vast majority of students went home at the end of each day. A constant reminder for many of us of the fact that LCC had boarders was a gigantic dull grey metal tube, four feet in diameter, which descended from the top floor of the building just outside the windows of the AV room. This monstrosity served as the emergency fire escape, essential in particular for the boarders due to the absence of exits at the back of the building. Although it was taboo, nefarious individuals would nevertheless take the opportunity to try it out. Unfortunately for them it was not a smooth ride, as inside the chute there were rough ridges where the sections had been crudely joined. On top of this there was a mass of accumulated dust and dirt and also quite a significant drop to the ground from the end of the pipe.

Those of us from that era will also remember the school Chef, a most amazing man who looked after our dietary needs. That vibrant character was Chef Richard (Dick) de Grandpré and the School was very fortunate indeed to have had his lifetime of service. Our days at LCC were enhanced by his keen sense of humour, and he even managed to find levity in such pranks as the one where some mischievous boarders left a single sausage on each of the steps on the (now defunct) staircase that led up to the top floor from the kitchen. It would seem that the senior boarders were demonstrating their displeasure through meat products of new restrictions imposed by an overly zealous Boarding Master, who had outlawed their late evening toast-making sessions.

A dedicated staffer, Dick prepared all the required meals and provided whenever he could some little extras for the staff. I remember one night he stayed late to prepare an unexpected supper for Steeve Lee and myself as we laboured long into the evening to gear-up for that year's History Night.

When Dick was a young man in the 1950's, he would arrive early in the morning on his powerful motorbike. With only a very limited budget to work with, he still created miracles with the food. He was an "Old School" chef – there were no pre-made meals or powdered gravy mixes that could be added to hot water. Rather, he would painstakingly cut the meat off the bones and slow-boil them overnight in the kitchen's giant cauldrons to make the stock. His time and effort showed, as lunches at LCC were better than many a home-cooked meal.

When I was a student, meals were served on LCC-crested china imported from England. There were seldom seconds; what was on the platter had to feed the students at your table, so some tables with hungry eaters (like me) cued up for the leftovers from the tables with more modest appetites. Each table had eleven students with a Master presiding and each week student waiters served in an on-rotation basis, duly dressed in a starched white coat, which was either too small or too large for our assorted body types. They were responsible for collecting the food, clearing the cutlery and dishes and then wiping the table clean at the end of the meal. When in this position there was never sufficient time to eat, so all of the waiters ate following the main meal. When it got to be my turn to serve, I noticed that Chef de Grandpré always looked after his waiters by providing them with a larger platter of meat and more gravy. In other words, you were compensated for your efforts and dined well.

A day that I won't forget was our last luncheon. Now called the Graduate Luncheon, the grade eleven graduating class and Staff would convene in the Dining Room for a final up-scale meal. It was the one occasion when the students had the honour to sit interspersed with their teachers, who have always been the greatest strength of LCC. This was a happy occasion, but nevertheless tinged with sadness, as you looked around the room and realized that after having spent many years together we would never again be together as a group.

### Teachers of Character and Rotten Carrots

In many ways, my grade seven teacher Mr. Geoff Merrill was like a second father. I could write a book about Geoff Merrill, but the best stories

I could never put into print. However, I will include one favourite anecdote.

I had been away with the flu and had missed several days. In my absentee note, my mother told Mr. Merrill that I had been like a "caged lion" and wanted to get back to his classroom very badly. When it came to food, Geoff had one great love and one thing which he absolutely detested: with his sweet tooth he could not resist chocolate, but on the other hand he detested carrots. The day before I was to return to school, I had found some rotten old carrots in our pantry, which considering their state, must have sat there undetected for several months They were mouldy and had almost liquefied, with green fuzz covering the outside and a runny purple ooze within. So I mischievously prepared an enormous piece of fudge and encased the rotten carrots in the center.

When I returned to school the next day, I placed the huge piece of fudge on Mr. Merrill's desk. When he entered the classroom, he noticed the fudge and asked who had brought it. I raised my hand in confirmation and requested that he eat the fudge in the character of Doris Clark, one of Montreal's celebrated radio personalities of the time and a true representative of the old "Montreal Establishment". In other words, he was to make 'much ado' about the fudge, and then in a not-so-genteel manner, demolish it in one bite. This he did with such gusto that the students in the first three rows were sprayed with fudge and chunks of rotten carrot, proof that the decayed vegetables had found their mark.

In those days, students wouldn't normally dare try stunts like that on their unsuspecting teachers, but Mr. Merrill was so surprised that I actually got away with it. The next day, I brought him a whole box of fudge squares. All the while looking in my direction, he again asked who had brought in the fudge. I raised my hand, but assured him that this time it was the Real McCoy. He took one look at my innocent smile, and figured it best to send me to the kitchen and get a fork and then made me eat a piece which he chose at random to prove that it was untainted. In spite of this, he gingerly pronged each piece with the fork before he ate it; but the fudge was good and all was forgiven.

For all his bravado, Geoff was a very sensitive man. One day he responded to a student's question as to whether he had any regrets in life by recounting to us how his mother had died at a young age, suddenly and totally unexpectedly. He had very much loved his mother, but had never expressed this to her or thanked her for all she had done for him. He said that he had always felt regret and guilt that he had not done so, and by then it was too late. I learned something very important from him that day, and when my father was terminally ill with cancer, I poured out my love and thanks to him in a letter. Shortly before his death, Dad wrote me back. After his passing, I found it amongst his private papers. My father may well not be with me physically, but to this day I feel the spirit of the love between us embodied in those two letters. I thank Geoff for pointing me in the right direction so that I did not miss that important opportunity.

Geoff Merrill taught me the joy of learning and how to fully embrace my childhood, as he was a great believer in letting kids be kids. Because of him, I have encouraged each of my students to live out their youth to the fullest. This can be difficult in today's society, as children are pushed along too quickly to become nothing more than little adults. This leads to many "young" adults not only being deprived of, or shortening, their childhood experiences, but also taking much longer to mature than we did. Admittedly, our lives were more structured and straightforward, but there is a price to pay if you try to short cut the growing-up experience, which can result in children maturing without any joy.

In spite of all his wisdom, Mr. Merrill was also very human, and was not immune to the occasional case of foot-in-mouth syndrome. On one particular day he entered our classroom and announced that his close friend, Mr. Dave Wood, and his wife had just had a son. A vexed expression came over his face as he told us that they were going to call the young boy Bruce. Mr Merrill continued, "I am really happy for Mr. Wood, but I can't believe that they are going to call him Bruce. It is not the greatest of names to choose." At that moment there came a loud throat- clearing from one Bruce Jenkins seated at the back of the class, who obviously was not all that amused. Geoff quickly back-pedaled and tried to recover by stating, "Of course, once the lad gets to be eleven or twelve, then Bruce is a great name." It was one of the few times that I saw him with egg on his face. He may have had faults that would occasionally trip him up, but his sincerity, caring for his students and zest for life made him an invaluable role model.

I was hyperactive, always getting into trouble, and my reports were nothing to write home about. However, I could play a half-decent game of hockey in the nets, and my game was modelled after my idol, the legendary goalie Jacques Plante. I lived for hockey, as it was an activity wherein I could hold my head high amongst my peers. With great coaches and wonderful players in front of me, the result was that we usually won. It is fitting that the defining moment of my high school career was to occur following one of my senior hockey games. Geoff Merrill was no doubt the teacher who had the greatest influence on me as I went through the school. This is encapsulated perfectly in an incident that occurred late in my high school days and gave me the courage not to give up.

It was March, and I had just received my report card – the worst report card that I had ever received, in fact, the worst report card that I have ever seen. Even my history mark was down. My teachers were discouraged with my performance and even my saintly mother was losing faith in me. I was on the verge of giving up on myself, and when a student gives up on him or herself, it's all over! Graduating from high school now seemed unimaginable at that point in time, and how was I going to become a teacher without a university education? I was so frustrated! I knew I wasn't stupid, but I just couldn't seem to demonstrate my intelligence. Fully expecting to be asked to leave LCC at that juncture, I was in a state of utter frustration and depression. Why couldn't I achieve like everyone else?

I was standing in front of my locker late Friday afternoon, having just finished a hockey game. Suddenly, there was a tap on my right shoulder and I turned around, half expecting some prank from one of my peers. Instead, it was Geoff Merrill. "I have just read your report card," he said. I thought to myself. *Oh! No! Not you, too!* Geoff put both of his hands on my shoulders and held me firmly, looking me straight in the eyes.

"Forget it," he said, "I know you, and you will be successful. Just roll up your sleeves and come back in here on Monday morning and get back to work."

"But…but…but my report card," I said.

"No buts," he said, "Give me that report card and I'll tear it up. You will eventually make it. You will be successful. Now just go home and relax this weekend, and come back to school on Monday, refreshed and ready to get down to work."

Boy! Did I ever need that! On the verge of becoming a high school dropout, there was still one person who had not given up on me. I don't think that I would ever have endured if Geoff Merrill had not spoken to me that day – my father was already speculating about finding me a job. I did come back on that Monday, renewed, refreshed and ready to try my best once again. Over the next two years my overall average went up considerably and I went on to become an honours history student at university. The influence that a teacher possesses to help make, or break, the spirit of a student can be the turning point in either direction of an academic life and I was lucky enough to have the complete support of such an individual, someone who would not let me give up on myself.

Fortune shone on me in other ways as well, as I was able to count on the wisdom, advice and genuine support of our Headmaster, Dr. Stephen Penton, during my last three years at LCC. He was a noble man who cared very much about all of his students, not just those obtaining first class honours. Dr. Penton always considered the total individual, not just the student's academic performance: What kind of person were you? Did you believe and try to follow the precepts of the School's motto *Non Nobis Solum*? Were you a credit to your family, yourself and the School?

I had toiled for eight years at LCC, but beyond a doubt grade ten was my hardest year. We carried all the subjects for both Arts and Sciences, and that was *operation overload* for me. Physics, chemistry, biology, algebra, trigonometry, geometry and 200 marks for Latin, and that was just to start! At the end of grade ten I was asked to meet with Dr. Penton in his office. "What are we going to do with you, Denny?" he said with a smile. I replied that grade ten had been extremely challenging, but I thought that I could do better in grade eleven. The number of subjects was reduced, there were fewer maths and sciences, and no more Latin. Furthermore, I could take an extra history course. "And you are not getting any younger, and the senior hockey team needs their goalie." It was certainly a respectable way of saying that you are too old to repeat grade ten, which several students did that year.

Years later, with my wife's blessing, we named our son Stephen after him. Ironically, Dr. Penton and I are both named Denys Stephen, and while our son bears my name, he is not named after me but rather this remarkable educator and revered third Headmaster of LCC.

My time in high school was a combination of small triumphs and many major frustrations. Oftentimes my inappropriate behaviour was a smokescreen to hide my academic difficulties and certainly my poor reading skills were to blame. I enjoyed reading occasionally, when I found an author that I liked, but usually I would stumble across a good book rather than searching one out. My tape-recorder mind may have been outstanding, but my note-taking skills, such as being able to discern what was really important as opposed to what was interesting, were lacking. So I compensated by resorting to my usual classroom antics with my teachers; funnily enough it was usually the teachers that I cared about, rather than those I disliked, that were routinely challenged.

### An Eccentric Teacher Can Make a World of Difference

I had the late Ned Heney for English and geography. He was very much his own man, different and quite eccentric. Instead of personally correcting our tests, he would occasionally have the students correct each other's tests, but no one was allowed to question the mark the student marker reported on your behalf. An interesting system, and one I once felt compelled to challenge.

Geography was one of my stronger subjects and I could anticipate Mr. Heney's tests well. One such example was the day we were tested on the cities of the world. I guessed that Athens would be one of those cities, as my close friend Peter Wright had just moved to Athens, Georgia. We were all given a sample copy of the test map and I was easily able to locate it within a millimetre. Then I waited for my opportunity to shine. Needless to say the student marking my paper marked me wrong, just as I had anticipated. When the student announced my grade of 19 out of 20, I immediately called out,

"20 out of 20, Sir! I am sure my peer in question, not finding Athens in Greece, marked me wrong. There is also an Athens, Georgia, where I have correctly located it. You did not specify that Athens had to be in Greece, Sir! So my mark is 20 out of 20, not 19."

While I could have easily saved myself the hassle by simply choosing the more common answer of Athens, Greece, I was willing to go the extra mile in order to make my point and had proven to him that not being allowed a challenge to a student-marked test was unfair. I got my perfect score and I think that I earned a little respect from Mr. Heney for my efforts. After all, it was the kind of thing that he would have done himself.

Ned was someone I always looked forward to seeing at LCC Alumni events. He always had a particular twinkle in his eyes when he saw me and we would relive many of our moments shared both inside and outside the classroom, including our famed "Steam Train Excursion" from Montreal's Central Station to Victoriaville and back. One of my classmates, Geoffrey Southwood, had asked me if I would like join him and Ned on this trip and I accepted. We drove down to the station in Ned's Austin, which had a shelf below the dash board. We were intrigued by the unshelled hard-boiled egg that he had placed there as, unnoticed by Ned, the egg rolled back and forth across the shelf collecting all manners of dust and dirt. All of a sudden, Ned plucked it up and ate it. He had eaten this dirt-covered egg and hadn't even noticed he was so engrossed with the upcoming trip! We had known Ned to be eccentric, but he was a very different person out of the classroom. On that Saturday morning he was relaxed and unencumbered by classroom regulations, treating us as equals and not as his students.

The influence that a teacher has can be enormous. That simple Saturday excursion on a steam train, run outside official school hours, would spark Geoff Southwood's lifelong passion to learn everything possible about railways, trains and their history. So often in education, we learn or are inspired to seek knowledge by our relationships with our teachers outside of the classroom setting, and Ned Heney proved to be just such a catalyst.

That day was also the beginning of my lifelong friendship with Geoff Southwood. It is amazing how one event, or the shared camaraderie of one special day, can sometimes blossom into much more than you would ever have anticipated. Many years later, Geoff said to me,

> "You were the only one from the 'jock set' that would ever
> have deigned to do something other than sports. None of
> the other jocks would ever have gone on a "Steam Train
> Excursion". You were one of the jocks, but you were
> different."

Another teacher who was quite the character was Lionel O'Neill. He is probably best remembered by the boarders, as he used to run a full-length feature film on LCC's ancient projector every Wednesday evening for them. He was my principal high school history teacher and while poor on discipline, he was amazingly well read and he told the best historical anecdotes that I have ever heard. I especially enjoyed picking his brain outside the classroom. I worked hard for him as he praised me and he dubbed me his "Historical Encyclopaedia".

One of my classmates, Peter Eddison, could never understand how I could get marks like 3% in math, 21% in algebra and yet score 97% in history. He was a brilliant individual, who went on to earn the Governor General's Medal – awarded to the student with the highest marks in grade eleven. He was perplexed by my scattered academic triumphs – how was that possible with my overall standing? Quite simply, I really liked history, and really only applied myself to my history courses. Studying history wasn't work, it was a pleasure, and when I scored well, my teacher made me feel that I was special. I just did enough in my other subjects to scrape by. As Richard Branson would affirm, "If you're not interested, you can't grasp it!" (March 2007). At that stage of my academic life, history had clearly become my principal interest.

Reflecting back on my lifetime in education, I cannot emphasize enough the significance that passion does play in our dreams, our realities and our abilities.

Why is it that some students excel and others don't?

What motivates a student to be successful?

What gives a student that inner desire and strength to succeed?

Why do some students carry that aura of success about them?

The answer to all these questions (and many others) is *passion*; it is the key ingredient for lifelong learning. Passion is the greatest of all motivators! It drives us to explore fervently every aspect of our desired learnings, making them special and often inseparable from our lives. Passion gives us the courage to take steps that go beyond our perceived limitations. We are what we are, but passion will drive us to attain everything that is possible, and sometimes even more.

### Zero Tolerance

Without question, my passion for history was evolving. However, I was still confronted by an educational system in which I had to take many other less appealing subjects. Since I really wasn't motivated to learn (in the conventional sense), my usual response was some form of inappropriate classroom behaviour and even in my senior years, I still couldn't resist challenging some of my teachers.

The late Walter McBroom was my teacher for geometry and trigonometry in grades eleven and twelve. He was a very private man who quietly went about his business in a no-nonsense manner and often kept to himself, spending hours smoking and doing crossword puzzles in the staffroom. Nevertheless, he was one of the teachers most helpful to me when I joined the staff in 1970. At the time I was a little taken aback by his kindness, as I had on occasion not been too considerate of him.

As a teacher, he was very dry as he would simply present the material and set us to work. But he had one unusual habit, which was probably acquired in teacher's college – he never looked at his students directly when speaking in front of the class. Instead, he always focused his gaze to the back of the classroom, where the back wall met the ceiling. This was too much for me and one day I got out my Scotch tape, paper and black ink markers. I wrote a note in giant six-inch letters and posted it across the back wall just beneath the ceiling. It read,

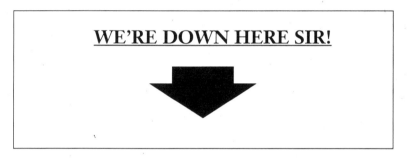

He was truly incensed and I was kicked out of his classroom and forced to serve a major detention. The funny thing is that Walter had a keen sense of humour, and I shared many a light moment with him as a colleague, but he was the sole master of his classroom and would tolerate no student interference or insolence.

### A Mathematical Dilemma

In grade twelve I had Mr. John Brown for Intermediate Algebra, which was undoubtedly my worst subject. I will never forget my first class with this man, who was among the most intelligent members of the LCC teaching staff. At the start of the year, he walked into our classroom and announced that we had a choice: he could get us all a minimum of 70% on our senior matriculation exam, or, he could teach us math. He paused and then stated that he had decided that he would teach us math.

Of course, this was not the answer I was looking for. I raised my hand.

"Yes, Mr. Heward, What is your question?" He said.

I looked at him very soberly, eye to eye, and said, "I'll take the 70%, Sir!"

"No, Mr. Heward!" was his response, "I'm going to teach you math!"

I never obtained my senior matriculation because of my math marks. However, three years later at university, I actually scored 100% on my math mid-term exam, so maybe he had planted a few seeds after all. Truth be told, during my time in university I had discovered that math is actually an easy subject to master. The trick is that you have to learn 100% of it; you can't beat the system by only learning part of it. You can half learn your history and by guessing right you can score a 95, but you can learn 90% of your math and still fail. It is all about the component parts. Each and every component must be learned and mastered in order to solve the problem. One missing link can spell disaster.

My first eighteen years as a teacher, I taught math to grades five and seven. While it was only at a junior level, I still really enjoyed the experience. I really felt for those students who struggled with the subject, and I am sure that I helped some students discover their latent mathematical abilities. My high school career was made miserable by my constant failing grades in math, but when I changed my approach out of necessity in university, I kicked myself for all the math marks that I had previously thrown away. Math may not be simple, but it isn't all that hard either; it just looks intimidating or frightening. Unless you are naturally mathematically inclined, it requires daily effort and work and you have to take the time and make the effort to study every piece until you have mastered them all. However, like a giant jig-saw puzzle, they all magically fit together.

### A Father's Concern

In September of 1966, I left the confines of LCC. After ten years at the School being helped along and encouraged by caring teachers and supportive classmates, it was time for me to forge ahead on my own. My parents felt that going away to university would be almost as much of a learning experience in itself. My father had been based in Halifax during World War II, and my mother had spent part of the war with him in Nova

Scotia. Thus, they insisted that I consider the smaller and more intimate maritime universities. There the class sizes were usually under thirty students and your teacher was actually the professor himself, not some teaching assistant.

In the mid 1960's, Mount Allison University and the University of New Brunswick were popular with some LCC graduates – they both had good reputations and were closer to Montreal than Dalhousie or Acadia. UNB had a reputation amongst my peers as being a good "beer drinking" college, but my parents (in particular my father) steered me away from there. They were in favour of the smaller, Baptist-influenced, tea-totalling Acadia University, situated in a truly beautiful location just off the banks of the Bay of Fundy in the Annapolis Valley.

My father was a good man, hard-working, decent, sincere and a strict disciplinarian. He was highly intelligent, but he had not been able to achieve his life's dream of becoming a medical doctor. At the dawn of the Second World War, he left McGill and spent the next four-and-half years as a Lieutenant Commander on the Corvettes, protecting the supply convoys travelling between North America and the British Isles. By the time the war was over, he had a wife and two children to support which meant he had to join the workforce rather than go back to university.

When I informed my father upon graduation from university that I had chosen to go into teaching, he threw me a dark stare and said, "Well, you'll never have that big house in Westmount, if you do!" On that score, he was right. My father, like so many of his generation, held beliefs that today would be considered politically incorrect. He was blunt and not afraid to speak his mind, however offensive such comments might appear today. He loved me and he wanted the best for me even if our lines of communication seemed closed on occasion.

I often felt that I was a disappointment to my father. He had such high expectations for me and wanted me to go into business with him. I, however, liked doing things my own way, and had no desire to become an accountant or a businessman. My father had a difficult time adjusting to the way I did things. He could not understand why I was not doing what he wanted me to or doing it the way he wanted. But I am indebted to my father for providing me with such an outstanding example of community service, and for entrusting me with his philosophy of life: "Take everything you can out of life, and live life to the fullest, but always make sure to give back just a little more than you take out!"

A good example of the dynamics of our relationship occurred the night I left for Acadia. Just before I was to board the train at Westmount Station, my father put out his hand which I took in my own, looked me straight in the eye and said, "Do the best you can, son, and don't worry, I'll help you get a job next year." My father loved me, but his well-meaning but misguided statement crumpled my fragile ego. I thought to myself, even my own father doesn't think I am going to succeed.

My father never earned his degree. He lived his life larger than life, a tough guy, standing 6'3" and weighing 250 pounds. And yet, for all his gruff and tumble demeanour, he still had to leave the auditorium choked up with emotion and tears when I received my diploma at Acadia four years later.

# Chapter Three
## Thrust into the Driver's Seat

Like many men of my generation, I desired a happy marriage with a wife and children to come home to every evening. Furthermore, I wanted a life and a career which allowed me to be myself, use my creativity and be personally accountable for my actions. While I strove to reach these goals, fate turned out to play a major role in their fruition, as my father was diagnosed with colon cancer. His first operation went well, but unbeknownst to us at the time, the cancer had already spread to other parts of his body. He was never told the truth, but my mother and I knew that he only had a year or so to live. Having just spent the previous five years away at university I had spent barely any quality time with my dad or family. To make up for lost time, I decided to return to Montreal and to find employment so as to be closer to home.

In December of 1969, I met with Mr. Merrill (then Headmaster at LCC), and explained my situation. I inquired if he knew of any school board that would hire me to do substitute teaching, since I did not have any formal teacher training. I never even imagined that without official certification I could be hired as a full-time teacher, and surprised when Mr. Merrill inquired if I would be amenable to teaching grade five at LCC, starting in September. Grade five? I had envisioned myself teaching history in grades ten, eleven and twelve, and replied with a smile, "Don't you have to change diapers in grade five?" Mr. Merrill said that starting my career in the lower grades would really help me to learn the ropes, and besides, I could always move up to the higher grades later on if that was my interest. In any case, he informed me that my absence of a teaching certificate would be less of an issue in the Lower School.

In May of 1970, I received a phone call from Dave Wood, my former coach and teacher, now Director of the Junior School. He told me that he had my contract on his desk, and asked when I was coming to Montreal to sign it. Furthermore, I was offered the opportunity to spend three days assisting and observing in the class of a young master, Mr. Victor Badian. Since I had never spent an actual day as a teacher and had several days off before starting my summer job at Molson's Brewery, I readily accepted.

Vic and I had been students together at LCC, although he had been two or three years ahead of me. Now in his third year of teaching, he was young, dynamic and totally dedicated to his students. Throughout our years at LCC, we were to become the best of friends.

Under his encouraging and constructive eye, Vic kindly allowed me to do most of the teaching over those three days. While I learned a great deal from him in that short period, there was so very much more to come over the years that followed. On my third day of practice teaching, Vic said that I could teach all the periods that day, except one: he was going to teach the history class, as that was his favourite. We developed an immediate bond during those first few days together as we greatly appreciated many of the same things, especially a passion for history. For the bulk of the next thirty-five years, we would become the dynamic history duo of LCC's Middle School (grades 7&8). As Vic recalls, "Knowing Denys' love for history, I knew even back then that if I gave him the opportunity to teach my history class, I might never get it back."

The summer of 1970 was long and hot as I fulfilled my duties working the night shift at Molson's, cleaning out machines and performing jobs at every point of the bottling line. You were entitled to a free beer at lunch and after your shift, and every month each employee could purchase ten cases of 24 at $2.38 a case. Was I ever popular with my friends at our weekend parties! The summer passed quickly and soon it was time for my first official day as a teacher at LCC. I rushed up those front stairs for the first time as a teacher, my racing heart a reminder of my excitement. Standing by the main door was one of my former French teachers, Monsieur Jean-Pierre Cruvellier. He reached out his right hand in friendship and while touching my shoulder with his left, he looked me in the eyes, smiled and said, "Welcome to the Staff, Heward. I hope they give it to you like you gave it to us." At least he smiled! In reality, I was very pleasantly surprised at how well I was treated by many of my old teachers. I had certainly given them a hard time, and here they were being nothing but kind and helpful to me. There were a few twinges of guilt now and then, but they passed quickly as I had enjoyed my teacher-baiting years.

While it was nothing to write home about structurally, that beloved building on Royal Avenue would become my second home for the next thirty-five years. I enjoyed, indeed loved, going to "work" throughout my career, as each day with my students was an adventure. In all those years I think I took only eight sick days, and half of them were before I was married (three years after I started teaching). My students gave purpose to my life. They taught me so much about the modern world, and they kept me young of heart and mind, body and soul.

### Lessons Learned

I have always believed that good teaching requires dialogue, for if you take the trouble to listen to your students' thoughts and concerns first, they just might listen to you. Or, in the more concise words of educator Thomas Lickona, "First you reach'em! Then you teach'em!"(85). A teacher that is only interested in imparting his or her own views and cannot or will not hear what their students have to say is not likely to make a significant impact. It is not enough to simply be an expert in your field of study – you have to be able to ignite a fire within each of your students for them to want to learn, and establishing open communication is a great way to start.

No teacher can do the learning for his or her students; they have to do it for themselves. Rather, your job as an educator is to gain their trust and confidence and to ignite their inner desire to want to learn. Once that is established, you can make constructive suggestions to guide them in the right direction, suggesting alternatives and avoiding pitfalls along the way. Once your students are motivated and actively engaged, nothing can hold them back. You have passed the torch!

If it weren't for the cumbersome red tape of the administrative process, I would teach until the day I die. All I have ever wanted was to share my love of history with an engaged and willing audience, and hopefully my students have grown to appreciate history and learning as much as I have. Being in a classroom interacting with positive students is a pure and exhilarating experience. I cannot think of any other place where I would rather spend my day.

That first day, as I walked through the long halls of LCC, I barely felt older than the Senior Academic Year (students of grade twelve). I reported to the office for any last minute instructions from Dave Wood, the Junior School Director. He smiled the knowing smile of a veteran looking with sympathy at a totally raw rookie, gave me a great big pile of books and pointed at my classroom door. "Go in there and teach, my boy, and remember, be tough! Be fair, but be tough!"

With Dave's words ringing in my ears, I entered my classroom for the first time and encountered twenty-seven smiling faces. Almost all of that first year is forever etched in my memory, probably because every step was a learning experience. Nothing was 'old hat'; everything was new and each successive day brought about different challenges as I tried things for the first time. Thank goodness for those three days the previous May in Vic Badian's classroom, but even that seemed ages ago. I was lucky that my first class was, for the most part, an exceptionally good group of ten-year-olds and the first morning was traditionally reserved for the homeroom teacher.

In the early 1970's, LCC had added a full class at the grade five level, which meant that at least half of my students were new and full of anxiety with their own first day jitters. So I spent that first class soothing their nerves, providing orientation, organizing textbooks and schedules, making introductions, renewing acquaintances and setting out the school rules and expectations. I stayed true to Mr. Wood's recommendations and set a tough tone, but as my students got to know me they would realize that was not my normal style. In truth, by lunchtime I was beginning to feel uncomfortable with my tough guy act – I didn't want my first charges to go home to tell their parents that they had an ogre for a teacher!

However, my uneasiness brought about a tradition that I started that first morning and continued for the next thirty-five years: "Questions you have always wanted to ask a teacher but never dared!" Alas, on that first morning I had yet to add the proviso, "but within the realm of good taste and respectability." There were just a few minutes left before the end of the third period and this seemed like a good way to hopefully start up a two-way communication between my students and myself. Of course, by not giving my students any guidelines I had set myself up big time. After some hesitation, a lone brave hand went up in the back of the classroom.

"What is your question?" I asked.

"Sir, do you like women with 'big boobies'?"

His father was a gynaecologist so I should have seen it coming, but I was a raw rookie. This was a first day learning experience and it completely caught me off guard. Thinking on my feet, I replied, "That question will remain unanswered this morning, but as you get to know me, the answer will be self-evident."

Over my thirty-five years, if ever I had a few minutes remaining at the end of my class, I would open the floor to my students for any interesting questions they might have had. While sometimes frivolous, I would frequently get provocative questions that would give me the opportunity to open up a dialogue with my students on topics that were of interest to my students, but which they seldom had the occasion to discuss with an adult. It may have been pedagogically risky, but I have never regretted the decision.

### Almost a Short Career

As parents paid a sizeable sum to send their sons to LCC, there were certain expectations. At the very least, I was supposed to be fully qualified and my lack of formal training certainly increased my anxiety in my first years of teaching. However, I did take my official teacher training over the next three summers at McGill University, much to the relief of the administration. I became certified before the government inspectors could make too much of a fuss, but at least now the School could argue on my behalf that I was actively involved with the process of teacher certification.

I taught English, math and Canadian history to the grade fives, as well as one of the four sections of British history offered in grade seven. While I enjoy teaching all subjects, I have a special place in my heart for history and I was always looking for ways to bring the subject to life. Over the next few years I developed a personal history curriculum. "History Through Characterization", which would eventually include an annual History Night put on by students (and some faculty). I enjoyed taking risks as a teacher, all in the name of capturing the attention and interest of my students.

My first idea was to re-enact a "Trial by Ordeal" from the depths of Anglo-Saxon England, where guilt or innocence was not decided by the courts but by God. It went really well but, much like the real thing, it was not a quiet affair and I was not aware as to how paper thin the classroom walls were. And so, while one unfortunate grade seven student was on trial for his life in my classroom, Mr. Allen Wightman's geography class was writing an important test in the adjacent classroom.

Following Mr. Wightman's complaint, I made my first trip as a teacher to the office of the Director of the Junior School, a place I had come to know well as a student. It was therefore no surprise that I felt a sense of foreboding as I entered the office, but Mr. Wood was very decent about the situation. He pointed out that "We can't have other classes disrupted during their tests," and he went on to suggest that I find quieter ways of delivering my material. While I knew that as a rookie I had better follow the regime until I could find my way, I never wanted to just toe the line. I made it my goal throughout my career to continually attempt to reach my classes by employing methods that were out of the ordinary. However, from that day forward if my unorthodox methods meant an increase in volume, I had the good sense to take my students out of my classroom to the field or some more soundproof area.

### Guilty as Charged

In my first year as a teacher I soon came to realize the immense influence a teacher can have on his students and how even the most innocuous of comments can have an enormous effect. A case in point was the story of my total aversion to Cream of Wheat. When I was a young boy, my dear mother would usually make my breakfast and on several occasions, she served me the cereal in question. Unfortunately, it was not cooked properly and thus was full of mucus-like lumps – in short, it was disgusting! However, whenever I resisted I would be lectured on how two thirds of the world's population was starving, and how dare I complain about the food that was being put in front of me. Finally, I said to my mother, "Ok! When you would be serving me Cream of Wheat, don't serve me anything for breakfast and I will go without food that morning. Count the days and when I would have eaten that whole box, – send it to them!"

Naturally, this is the type of story I would share with my students, full of embellishments, and the kids seemed to enjoy the story as much as I enjoyed telling it. I did not think that it would have any lasting impact. However, at my first parent teacher evening, I was accosted by an irate mother.

"Mr. Heward, I really appreciate you as my son's teacher, but I have a bone to pick with you. For years, I have been serving my son Cream of Wheat for breakfast on a regular basis. Now he refuses to eat it. He simply pushes the bowl back at me and says, "Send it to them!" I gather from my son that you are the culprit."

*Mea Culpa.* I know that Cream of Wheat is a nutritious food, but to this day I still can't eat it and I could not in good conscience encourage my students to eat it either.

### A Teacher's Radar

While my behaviour at LCC as a student was less than exemplary, my ne'er-do-well days gave me an edge as a teacher, as I was able to detect mischief in almost any form from my students. There was little that they could do that I hadn't done already (and quite possibly better!). Certainly most teachers have built-in radar for such situations, but mine was heightened by the fact that I had already committed each offence many times and in some cases, had nearly perfected it.

A good example of my keen sense for impending mischief occurred one day in my seventh grade history class, back in the days when LCC was still an all boys' school. One of my pupils was a spirited young man who preferred to sit at the very back of the classroom, usually in one of the middle rows of seats. While no slouch intellectually, he was more interested in participating in classroom antics than applying himself academically and thus did not meet his own potential. On this particular day he took his usual seat but for once actually had his history binder open, something he rarely did. Moreover, he was holding it up almost vertically, a far more awkward position for note-taking. How strange, I thought to myself, and then I noticed the furtive sideways glances from his peers who sat nearby. Not only did they continually look in his direction, their faces bore a mask of concealed pleasure – which led me to assume that the boy had a copy of *Playboy* magazine concealed behind his binder. I took no immediate action but instead continued to teach as if I was not aware of any wrongdoing.

As the period was ending, I moved down the side row to the back of the classroom and stood by the door that the boys would soon exit to go to recess. The guilty party was one of the first in line, flanked by an entourage of his peers; as he passed me to exit the class, I put my hand on his shoulder and stopped him. Whilst he attempted his best look of feigned innocence, I calmly but loudly stated for his fellow peers to hear: "I liked the brunette on page twenty-eight much better than the blonde that you were looking at." His face fell; the ruse was up. We walked in silence to my office. Once there, I made it clear to him that his work to date was in no way satisfactory and that he had an important decision to make. Either I could call in his parents so that he could explain as to why he was reading a copy of *Playboy* in class, or he could buckle down and prove to me that he could be as good as his potential suggested. If he decided upon the latter, the matter of the magazine would be dropped – so long as he kept up his end of the bargain. I informed him that should he renege, I would immediately dispatch a letter to his parents explaining what had happened. I never had to write that letter as his improvement was remarkable.

### Once-in-a-Lifetime

In 1971 Montreal experienced a record breaking winter, when snow piled higher and higher with each successive snowfall. This was also coupled with bouts of freezing rain, which seemed to turn the world to glass. During one such storm the rain had left a thick coating of ice across the entire LCC field, one that could withstand your body weight on skates – essentially one giant, perfect skating rink. It was such a unique opportunity that I couldn't resist arranging to take my grade five class out for a skating period, one I hoped they would never forget. Upon asking permission, I was informed by the powers that be that there needed to be a purpose for such an activity period. Such things could not just be undertaken for fun! So I quickly concocted a few velocity, wind power and ice friction experiments so that I would justify taking my boys out to the field. For fifteen minutes, we conducted our "experiments" and carefully recorded our data on small pads, with some stop-watch times thrown in for good measure. Once it looked like my students had learned something, we took off on our skates across the field for the rest of the period.

It was thrilling for me to skate an entire lap around the LCC field and to use the Carolina poplars which marked the border of the westward field as giant pylons, darting in and out, all the while pursued by twenty-seven exuberant boys. Other winter storms would coat the field in ice, but it was the only time that the ice was thick enough for the field to become a makeshift arena, and I was thrilled to be able to share this once in a lifetime opportunity with my 5B class. While I was given a small slap on the wrist for bending the School rules, as my "experiments" were a total sham, deep down I believe that the administration understood that this occasion was special. In truth, they should just have taken the morning off and given every class that glorious opportunity.

## Pillows Are Not Just For Pillow Fights

For the next thirteen years, I taught grade five and gradually took over the teaching responsibilities of all four sections of the British history course taught in grade seven. During those years I relished both the enthusiasm of my students and the opportunity I was given to introduce so many new boys to the ways of LCC. There are certainly many incidents from my early teaching days I could recount here, but I have decided instead to focus on just two.

As a teacher, I seldom sat in my teacher's chair; instead, I usually stood at the front or paced around my classroom. When I did sit, it was usually on the edge of my desk. Unfortunately, the rough hewn edges of the wooden desks did not make for the best seat, as they would produce the odd splinter. This fact was not overlooked by my students and one morning I was presented with a home-made foam pillow upholstered in a green tartan material. It was a wonderful gift, which made my perch more comfortable and eliminated the possibility of catching my slacks on the rough edges of the desk.

Over time my students requested that they also be permitted to use pillows, a request to which I eventually agreed. Their cushions were in their desks and were used when we were having a more interactive teaching session, such as during English or history lessons. It was quite a sight to see all twenty-seven of my students perched on the top of their desks, and I think they concentrated better when in this mode, yet they never abused the privilege. My students realized that they were being given a special privilege, something that was never afforded to them in their other courses.

Students truly respond well to being given extra benefits and more often than not enjoy these bonuses without taking advantage. During my time as the Assistant Director of the Junior School, whenever I needed student volunteers I would often set up shop in the staffroom, a room that was traditionally out of bounds to them. They really enjoyed the treat of seeing where and how the teachers spent some of their free time and on occasion, students would volunteer for after-school work simply to have the experience of being allowed in the staffroom.

My first students will remember that this pillow was a trademark of my early years as a teacher. I can still clearly remember the day the Teacher

Certification Inspector came to visit my class. That day, I informed my students that in the afternoon a visitor was coming to class to watch me teach and that they shouldn't be concerned, but rather carry on as normal, which is exactly what they did. The second period of the afternoon was history and as the bell rang my students put away their math books and took out their cushions. Within moments, all twenty-seven students were seated on their desks. I gasped for a second as I was not sure that the Inspector would approve, but in any case, it was too late. Fortunately, she saw that this innovation in no way detracted from their concentration. My methods may have surprised her, but she soon warmed up to my style and wrote up a positive report about my teaching and classroom strategies.

### "I Don't Know If You Reached That Young Boy, But You Sure Reached Me!"

In my first year of teaching, I had a student in my homeroom with a quick mind and a wonderful sense of humour. He also had the uncanny ability to read my mind, and catch inferences in my comments that were not always appropriate for a student-teacher relationship. Oftentimes when I made a statement that could be interpreted in a more interesting way, I would see him sitting there with that special grin of his and immediately he had me thinking the same thing. One afternoon I actually had to ask him to leave my classroom as we were both laughing so hard over one of these "inferences"; he hadn't done anything wrong, but I couldn't regain my composure with him sitting there so I asked him to take "10" and then return.

His father was my allergist and I enjoyed his family. While much was expected from this young man, at times he could be a little too lacka-daisical. That year, his December report card showed that he was not living up to his potential, and so I decided early in the New Year to pull out all the stops and arrange a meeting with his family and another of his teachers, Mr. Bob Warrendorf. I even managed to secure the Director's Office for the occasion.

I had a special bond with this boy, as he had written me a very caring note in regard to the passing of my father. The note touched me and I promptly replied; his mother later told me that he carried my note with him in his blazer pocket at all times.

During the meeting I laid out the facts, but I still wasn't getting my point across. I decided to stop pulling my punches and said, "You know you have got to make a more determined effort in school and be prepared to stand on your own, because you never know when you might lose your father. We all hope to have our parents in our lives for many years, but that can change overnight." I continued my sermon for a little longer, and then noticed out of the corner of my eye tears welling up in Bob Warrendorf's eyes. We were both in our first year of teaching, and we were inexperienced with meetings such as the one we were hosting. When the meeting was over and the family had left the office, Bob approached me and said, "I don't know if you reached that young boy, but you sure reached me!"

### Saturday Detentions

There are a great many ways to exert control in a classroom. You can either be tough or you can kill them with kindness and show your students the compassion, love, and respect that you expect from them in return, but you can never fool your students. I have never been an advocate of the 'stick', and I avoided it as much as I could when I first joined the staff at LCC in 1970. In my early days of teaching I was given a lot of unsolicited advice, such adages as "go in there and be tough. You are not to be their friend" and "Control and strong discipline are at the root of good teaching. Always be fair, but you are the boss." My colleagues were well meaning and I appreciated the gesture, but with time and practice I found my own way of dealing with my students. My solution was to bring a wayward student in on Saturday. It of course meant that I too would lose a day of my weekend, but it was a tactic I only had to employ a few times a year to get my message across.

"John! Do you want to come in on Saturday to do your work, or do you want to settle down and do it now?"

"Thank you Sir, I'll do it now!"

Once the students knew that you meant business and would bring them in, they appreciated the second chance to avoid the Saturday Detention. When I did bring in a student or, when needed, a group of students, I would often give the students an in-depth grammar class with which I would take my time (after all I had all morning) and give them meaningful direction. It was not only the troublemakers who took part; I would also often invite any student who needed help to come in on a voluntary basis. They had to stay the whole time, but as they were not in detention and they could come in casual dress and were allowed to bring a snack. Over the years I was surprised by how many students took advantage of my 'extra help classes,' coming in on a Saturday morning when they didn't have to, and I never had a parent complain.

There was only one time that I knowingly abused the system. I certainly felt guilty about it, but it had to be done. I had a wonderful student in my grade seven homeroom who came from a delightful Spanish family that lived across the street from us on Royal Avenue. Our children were great friends and our families often socialized together, even travelling to Spain together. My students were aware of my friendship with this family, and so I had to send a message to my students that while I might know one student better than another, I still did not play favourites.

I addressed this issue with his family and they understood completely – this student would have to be given a Saturday Detention. This was easier said than done as this individual was a very polite, courteous and diligent student. For six weeks I tried to find some fault worthy of the punishment. When I realized that it just wasn't going to happen, I would have to create a pretext.

The opportunity arose after I had given my class a major spelling test, which for the most part was done poorly. Even the student in question had made two or three mistakes, though not as many as some of his peers. Nevertheless, that was it and he was in for it. Some students clued into the fact that while they had done worse, it was this particular student who had to go to Saturday Detention. Clearly, Mr. Heward did not play favourites. I had to do it and it worked.

Recently I had dinner with this alumnus in Madrid, where he is now teaching English. I reminded him of the Saturday Detention that he had served some years before and apologized to him, explaining that he had been a victim of a conspiracy concocted by his parents and myself. Until that day, he hadn't a clue that he had been set up so that he would not be regarded unfairly by his peers.

Even a hint of favouritism can lead to unfortunate repercussions in a classroom. True gentleman that he was, he simply accepted his punishment even if he thought that I was being a little tough on him when he had only made a couple of errors. Preferential treatment is something that every teacher should do their utmost to avoid at all costs. You may have more to do with one student than another, but you must try to maintain an even playing field.

*The School, 1972*

*The famous Spitfire*

*UK tour medieval banquet in Cardiff Castle,*
*with Dora Parsons and Bill Moger, ca. late 70's*

*Alumni team in Denmark, 1976*

*With Paul Keyton, mid-1980's*

*Jean-Marie Rochette*               *Ron Dixon and his famous smile*

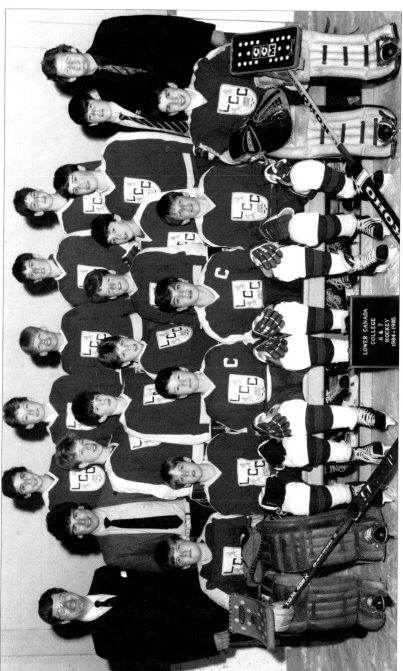

*Gr 6,7 Hockey Team, 1984–85*

*My corner*

*Old fire escape*

*With Mum and my wife Lyn*

*History Night, 1988*

*History Night S&E's, 1995*

*History Night, 1995*

*Two Elizabethan ladies, History Night, 2004*

# Chapter Four
## Lions

### *An Inspiring Individual*

There is always something to be learned from whatever happens to you, and even some of the most straightforward assignments can lead to unexpected surprises. In my first year, I was asked to coach the fall season of the eight-man House League tackle football team for Russel House. As a student, I had been in French House as had every one of my Heward relatives who had attended the School, and it almost felt like a betrayal to coach against my old house.

The four houses, Woods, French, Drummond and Russel, were each coached by a relatively new member of staff. Woods was coached by Ron Dixon, a native of Jamaica, whose passion was for science and biology although he had done some serious boxing along the way. He was a devoted family man with a wonderful sense of humour and a unique laugh. For many of us, working with Ron was also a learning experience as we had grown up, studied, worked and played in a Caucasian environment. Through Ron, we were exposed to a side of the world that we knew little about. The United States Congress had recently passed the Civil Rights Bill, and the 1960's had certainly shone a harsh light on the injustices inflicted upon blacks in North America. These were tumultuous times.

I like many others at LCC had grown up in a very sheltered environment, and for the first time my eyes were opened to some unpleasant realities in the world. Through discussions with Ron, I began to understand the meaning and consequences of discrimination and racial injustice. As I watched events unfold on my television in Montreal, the reality of the struggles occurring in such places as Selma and Montgomery, Alabama seemed so very far away. Surely, events like this couldn't happen here? Yet, if we don't heed the lessons of history, it takes but a single spark to ignite racial and political unrest anywhere, including in our own backyard.

### *Too Close For Comfort*

My first year of teaching coincided with the October Crisis in Montreal. The FLQ's kidnapping of two prominent officials, British High Trade Commissioner James Cross and Quebec's Vice-Premier Pierre Laporte, had thrown the city (and indeed the country) into such a state of panic that Prime Minister Trudeau invoked the *War Measures Act* and sent the army rolling into the streets of Montreal. Life went on but under the constant vigilance and presence of armed Canadian soldiers. There was also heightened security at LCC, as several of our children were from potentially targeted families. As Canada is normally a peaceful nation, we were not used to living under martial law, and I certainly never expected to have a machine gun thrust into my face.

One night during the crisis, I had gone to bed sick with the flu, my chest slathered with Vicks VapoRub. Arriving home late that evening, my younger sister Anne had stalled the family car at the entrance to our garage and had woken me up to see if I could get it started. At about 1:30 a.m., tousled and feverish I donned a plain grey tracksuit and went downstairs. To save the batteries, I decided to not turn on the car's headlights as I tried the ignition. Suddenly the car was bathed in bright light and I was literally a startled deer in the powerful searchlights of a military patrol. Within seconds the car was surrounded by soldiers and one of them was pointing a machine gun directly at my face.

"Who are you?" barked the soldier.

"I'm Denys Heward." I replied.

"Where do you live?"

"I live in the top floor duplex."

"Show me some identification," he commanded as he nudged the gun further into my neck.

"It's upstairs," I replied, "I'll go and get it." I tried to open the car door, which the soldier forcefully slammed shut.

"Don't move!" said the soldier gruffly.

In my sick and tired state, I had forgotten that the Army had set up one of its command posts at the local police station on the next block. I will never forget those moments of terror as the bright lights were aimed at me and a machine gun thrust in my face. When I look at events around the world today, I sometimes reflect on that one brief moment in our history and I am grateful for the fortune of having been born Canadian.

## Death Doesn't Take a Holiday

Over the years, I have made great friends and acquaintances, including that most inspiring individual Ron Dixon. We certainly enjoyed each other's company, and often laughed and joked together in the staffroom. However, Ron was not inclined to read important notices that were posted in the staffroom, which led to a situation which was undoubtedly embarrassing for Ron but quite beneficial for me.

Sadly, my father passed away from his struggle with cancer on New Year's Day 1971. Even though he had been sick for two years, his death came very rapidly catching the entire family off guard. With both funeral arrangements and the funeral itself to handle, I was unable to start the January school term on time and a notice had been posted in the staffroom to inform all of my colleagues of my father's death.

Although in some ways I was prepared, it was nonetheless difficult to accept the finality of my father's death. I was somewhat consoled by the fact that he had lived long enough to see that teaching was what I truly wanted to do, and that I was happily engaged in nurturing my young lads. While I was looking forward to being back in my classroom with the boys, I was dreading having to deal with the commiserations of so many sympathetic parents and colleagues. I know they meant well, and I just wanted some quiet, private time; but that was not to be.

Early that first morning back, I entered the School by the southern entrance and made my way down the long hallway to the reception area, the only other person in the hall being Ron, who was coming towards me. As I approached Ron, he suddenly grabbed me under my shoulders with both of his strong hands, lifted me off the ground and held me against the wall. I was so surprised that I didn't say anything and just hung there with my feet dangling. "School started three days ago, young man. What makes you so special that you can report back three days late?" It was just Ron's jovial way of saying "Happy New Year and I missed you over the holidays." I looked him straight in the eye and said, "My father died and I had to arrange his funeral." I will never forget Ron's face. He didn't know what to say or do. He just gradually lowered me to the floor, turned his back and slunk away without saying a word.

Once I got over the initial shock, I realized that I could probably face anything else that might happen that day. Ten minutes later, I hurried along to Ron's office to thank him for helping me to get back into the daily routine. I explained to him how nervous I had been that morning and wasn't sure how I would get through the day, but that his antics proved I really could face anything. Ron was such a gentleman and I knew that he felt terrible for his ill-advised actions. He hadn't read the notice and he didn't know that my father had died and he seemed so relieved that I had forgiven him, even thanked him, for what he had done. Many times over the years, we chuckled heartily about that early January morning incident.

I thought that I was in control of my emotions after receiving the condolences of so many of my colleagues, but I was caught completely off-guard by one of my students. It was the first period after morning recess and I was teaching English to my 5B homeroom class. In the midst of my explaining some particular point of grammar, one of my students, a wonderful boy who was usually very quiet, raised his hand and signalled that he had a question.

"Yes, can I help you?" I asked.

"Sir, did you know that they had a five-minute silence for your father at the Rotary Club luncheon yesterday?"

My father had been a proud Rotarian, and all his life he had been involved with many community service projects. As he had been unable to attend meetings during his illness, it had slipped my mind. This child's words meant so much to me at that moment and I could feel all of my emotions welling up within me, but in order to retain some composure I quickly turned the subject back to grammar. I can't remember if I ever thanked him for his kind remark, but I remember it as if it were yesterday.

### "You Really Don't Want to Look!"

When I look back over my life, I come to the realization that many of the things I did were done ass backwards. As a converted left-hander I ended up playing racquet sports, such as tennis and squash, with two forehands and no backhand. But that was only a minor difference. My pacing for other events in my life surpasses normal understanding, as I often found myself taking up activities ten years after most people would have stopped.

One of my great loves is hockey. If you attended LCC between 1955 and 2008, you most probably spent considerable time, as I did, playing hockey on our venerated ice rink. How I hated those blasted pigeons that nested in the rafters. Not to mention the indignity of having a healthy dollop of pigeon plop land on your head right after the opposition scored a goal into your net, as if to rub salt into the wound. I played nets throughout my time as a student at LCC, but at university hockey took a back seat to academics, although I still played when and where I could.

When I started teaching, I wanted to get the pads back on and get back into the net. However, I wanted to play serious hockey, competitive, yet without all the unnecessary fighting and dirty play, and so in 1972 I founded the Old Boys' Hockey League. The hockey was good and the alumni spirit excellent and I ran the league for twelve glorious years before finally hanging up my skates. I remember the night I decided that I had had enough. Vomiting and sick with the flu, I resolutely telephoned my fellow goalers in the hope of finding a replacement, only to discover that I was the third one to call. Thus sick as I was, I had to play not one game but two. Amazingly, I played well in the first game before fatigue and delirium took charge during the second.

At 38, with a young family and an exciting teaching career in full swing, I decided to sell most of my equipment to reduce the temptation of going back onto the ice. I held onto my old blocker and trapper as mementoes, partly because they were the wrong hand for most goalies but also deep down a part of me knew that I might some day need them. And, almost twenty years later, I discovered that my subconscious gesture had been right.

From the time that I "retired" from playing hockey I played only one game over the course of the next nineteen years. I had enjoyed my brief one-game return, but it wasn't enough to make me come out of retirement. That was left to the incomparable Ron Perowne. Ron had been LCC's Head Boy in 1967, and was, at the time of this anecdote, LCC's Director of Alumni Affairs. The alumni association was hosting a weekend tournament in January and some former elite players had formed a team called the "All Blacks". Ron was in desperate need of a goaltender and approached me to put on the pads.

In my heart I really wanted to play, but in the end, I decided to decline graciously. However, Ron is not one to give up so easily. On the day before the tournament, he beckoned me to leave my usual lunch table in the Dining Room to have lunch alone with him at a vacant table. "What is

your teaching schedule for this afternoon?" he asked, and I replied that I
had the last two periods of the day free. Of course Ron already knew that.
Ron had done his homework and I was being royally set up.

"I really want you to play for us this weekend."

"Ron, I have only had the pads on once in the last nineteen
years, I am out of shape, nursing a cold, and anyway I don't
have any equipment."

"So you are free the last two periods, you say? Why don't
we go out on the rink and I'll take some shots on you. Then
you can see how you feel."

"But I don't have any equipment," I said.

"No problem, I have already reserved the rink and I have
collected some equipment for you."

"But I catch with the right hand, Ron."

"I know. I already have your old gloves upstairs." As I said,
Ron doesn't take 'no' for an answer.

My son Stephen borrowed goalie pads and a chest protector from one
of my former students, as he didn't think much of the 'retro' pads with
which Ron had provided me. I was lucky that a barrage of screen shots just
managed to bounce off me in the first period; they actually made me look
more competent than I was. It was also the first time that my son had ever
seen me play, and that was quite a thrill for me. As the game wore on, I
gained confidence and the All Blacks actually won. My understanding had
been that I was to play only one game. I had not realized that there were
two more games on Saturday, and one on Sunday if we made the finals.
Saturday was one of those brutally cold days with temperatures at minus 25
Celsius. My block-glove hand froze within minutes of the start of the game.
That would teach me to use the gloves I had used in 1964! But the weather
did not hinder us and the All Blacks made it to the finals where I would be
victim of my own folly.

As I was a lot larger than my former student, his belly pad was too small
and really only covered half of my stomach. In the second period, one of
the fast young players on the opposing team suddenly rushed in on my
right side on a breakaway. Instinct told me to come out and cut down the
angle, and just at that moment he blasted a hard slap-shot at me. The puck
hit me full force on the right side of my midriff, right where there was no
padding. I felt the pain, but all I could think about was to pounce on the

loose puck and prevent a rebound. As I sprawled there on the ice, the feeling of discomfort began to seep in with a vengeance and I had to tell myself repeatedly, "You really don't want to look." We finished the game and retired to our dressing room. When I took off my shirt, I had a deep purple bruise, the size of a large grapefruit, on the right side of my stomach. For me all that mattered was that I had stopped the shot, but the bruise proceeded to turn a rainbow of colours over the next few weeks, and my alarmed wife kept saying: "No more hockey! No more hockey!" Well, I am still playing hockey, and sometimes when I am fortunate, with my son. No, I am not the goalie that I once was, but now I can really appreciate how Gordie Howe felt when he had the opportunity to play with his sons.

### A Life Extinguished Brings Hope for the Future

I'm sure that in all schools there are at least one or two favourite teachers that students and colleagues just enjoy spending time with. One such individual at LCC was Jean-Marie Rochette, one of the first French Canadians to be hired to teach French at the School. He was a young and inspiring teacher equally at home with the English and French-speaking teachers; quite simply for him, the "two solitudes" did not exist. Always armed with a great supply of jokes and stories, he was the one person that I could hardly wait to see in late August when the new school year was commencing.

December 19th, 1978 was the day of the annual Junior School Skate-a-thon. I just happened to have the period before lunch as a spare, and I sat in the staffroom laughing and joking with Jean-Marie for the entire time. Together we went for Chef Dick's annual pre-Christmas tourtière lunch, and then changed into our skates for our time on the rink with all 220 of the Junior School kids. Jean-Marie was a great skater, but he hadn't done much exercise of late. Sadly and somewhat prophetically, as he and I were standing at the top of the stairs leading down to the Dining Room, Mrs. Jean Power, the school nurse, walked by. Hoisting up his tattered skates by the laces, Jean-Marie saluted Mrs. Power and joked, "Don't go too far away, I may need your services in twenty minutes!"

The entire Junior School was on the rink, for the most part skating around slowly, with a few individuals darting about at a more rapid pace. Jean-Marie and I leaned against the boards half way to the blue line on the

Royal Avenue side of the rink nearest the School, watching the kids and chatting. After a while, he turned to me and said, "Well, it's time for me to go for a skate," and took off to his right, skating quickly towards centre ice. Ten seconds later, I turned and saw that he had fallen and I raced over to him. He was lying face down as I turned him over and saw a gash on his forehead. My first thought was that he must have tripped over one of the kids, falling and hitting his head, but I quickly realized that he was not breathing and feared the worst. I scanned the rink for Eric Lasota, our physical education teacher, who was much better acquainted with life-saving techniques than I was, and took the few seconds needed to get him, saying, "He needs CPR right away!"

As it was an extremely cold day I was wearing my great grandfather's racoon coat, which I took off and laid across Jean-Marie to keep him warm as I went to summon the nurse while Eric and the President of the Students' Council administered CPR. At that point I was still of the belief that his head injury was the problem, and I remember standing with a student who said, "There are only two people on the rink today who are not wearing helmets, Mr. Rochette and you, Sir!" Those words truly struck a chord and I have never again gone onto the rink without my helmet.

Jean-Marie had not tripped over a student. As we discovered later on, he had suffered a massive heart attack and was dead before his body hit the ice. All the valiant efforts to save him were in vain and Jean-Marie, who had just turned forty, was dead, leaving behind a loving wife and two young daughters. The entire LCC community, students, staff and teachers, were in shock. These things were never supposed to happen and certainly not to one of the School's most beloved teachers.

It was the worst Christmas that I have ever experienced as I was so upset by his death and funeral that I just couldn't summon any joy into my being. I was haunted by visions of his grieving wife and his two very young daughters, who just didn't understand why their father wouldn't wake up. Jean-Marie exuded a passion for life. He was one of the most loving people that I have ever known, and I think of him to this day. It was a tragic event that reinforced the fact that life can sometimes be very cruel. However, no matter the circumstances, we must continue on.

While you cannot prevent calamity or fool fate, you can learn from the hardships that are thrown upon you. More importantly, if you look hard enough, you can find some solace in tragedy. Over the years, in excess of fifty thousand dollars have been raised in memory of Jean-Marie Rochette for the Montreal Children's Hospital. We may not be able to bring him back, but his memory has brought hope and the chance for recovery for many children in need of critical support. His legacy lives on.

# Chapter Five
## Something Different

In my grade seven classes, I often employed some unorthodox methods to emphasize to my students when something was of considerable importance – information that they must retain. I had acquired a bugle when I had played the role of Teddy in *Arsenic and Old Lace*, and while I couldn't actually play this instrument, I was able to put my one note repertoire to constructive use.

When discussing study skills with my students, I pointed out that most teachers actually want you to pass their tests, or preferably do more than just pass. Thus, they will invariably give you large hints during their classes as to what is really important. Every teacher does it his or her own way, but the cues are always there. My method may have been eccentric but at the same time effective. In the middle of teaching, when I had stated something that I wanted my students to remember as being really important, I would open my desk drawer, pull out my bugle and blow one loud blast. And so, not unlike Joshua, who famously sounded his trumpet and the walls came tumbling down, I gave my students a signal that this material was guaranteed to be on a future test or exam.

Another tool in my musical arsenal was a family heirloom known as a *crécelle*. It is a wooden rattle that was also sometimes used as a liturgical instrument with incredible noise value, even louder than my trusty bugle. If I pulled out the *crécelle* and gave it a loud rattle, it was another way to signify to my students that the material I was discussing was important and most likely would be something they should know for upcoming tests. In either case, it certainly made any distracted students wake up and focus in a hurry.

Of course, I didn't want my students to learn just for the sake of learning, but also to enjoy the act of acquiring knowledge. Thus, I would actively encourage my students to read, not just because they had to, but to seek out books whose material was of high interest to them. However, when I mentioned that I would like to see them "reading for pleasure" each day, I was often confronted by the argument that this would be taking away from their television time.

So I struck up a deal – they could use their VCR's to tape their favourite shows, which could then be played back at the end of the evening as a way to unwind before bed. This gave them the added bonus of being able to fast forward through the commercials as well as allow them to go back and watch any super fantastic scene more than once. Two hours of recorded TV thus yielded over half an hour of reading time, without the loss of a single second of their beloved television programs. Many of my students adopted this practice, and some of my former students have since informed me that they are now employing this same system with their own children.

Regardless of whatever unusual techniques a teacher uses, it is imperative to have a principal who is courageous enough to stand behind your innovative methods. Most principals would be afraid of the possible flak they might have to endure, and so I count my blessings for a director like Paul Keyton, who tolerated and on occasion even encouraged my zany ways. To know Paul is to know someone who loves life; he was not a person to be intimidated by 'incidents' that were out of the ordinary. Paul's inspiration for teaching was so very evident in what he once told me: "When I began my teaching career with grade five at LCC, I made an inner pledge to myself that I would treat every boy as though he were my own child."

That mantra served me well in my years as a teacher, and helped me to reach some of the more difficult students. I encountered one such boy before he even set foot in my class. One day while teaching I was interrupted by a loud commotion in the hallway, as a dark-haired grade three student was in the process of unleashing a tirade of profanities upon his teacher. I didn't think that boys that age knew such words. I listened to the altercation and I formulated a plan. While this boy had a bit of a reputation, I had always found him congenial. That recess I went to see Paul Keyton and relayed to him the situation I had just witnessed, and then requested that this boy should be in my homeroom when he came to grade five.

"You want him in your class?" asked Paul with a quizzical look.

"Yes!"

"Why?"

"Because Paul, that kid has so much energy! If I can channel it in the right direction, can you imagine what kind of outstanding class leader he could become?"

My biggest investment in this lad was my time, and by the time he reached grade five he wanted to be in my class. He turned out to be one of the finest boys I ever taught at that level.

Spending as much time as I did in the classroom, I wanted to create learning experiences for my students outside of those four walls – something different and unusual that would captivate my students' imagination, a new type of experience that they would enjoy and long remember. The solution proved to be the two-week tours of the British Isles that another LCC teacher, Mrs. Dora Parsons, and I organized for many years over the March break. I had grown up living just a few doors down the street from Dora, and I had come to know her and her family well. When she sounded me out on the idea of doing such a tour, I leapt at the chance; what a wonderful way to pass on my love of history to a group of highly motivated students. Over the years I did twenty-two trips in all and enjoyed many wonderful experiences with my young travelling companions, who were given first hand access to the sites I had told them about in class. And for twenty-five years, we were honoured to share the company of Mr. Bill Moger, our coach driver from 1978 to 2003.

These trips allowed me not only to collect many wonderful anecdotes but also a fine selection of Irish Linen tea towels, which served as further educational tools in my classroom. Originally, my classroom had been part of the LCC boarders' quarters, hence there were many ugly pipes and even some old grey paint peeling off the upper walls and ceiling. As a paint job was not in the budget, I decided to literally wallpaper my classroom with tea towels, hanging them from the pipes and even suspending them from wires. At one point, I had over 275 of the colourful mementoes hanging in my classroom. It looked amazing! I remember one Parent Night when a concerned mother asked me if I was worried that my tea towels might be a distraction. I replied, "Madame! Even if a student daydreams in my classroom, he is still learning British history."

### Mary Had a Little Lamb

From 1977 to 2005, whenever someone had a birthday in my class, they had to stand up on their desk and sing "Mary had a Little Lamb". The story behind this bizarre tradition is this: in 1977 I had a particular student who was a great fellow, but very shy in front of his peers and averse to speaking in public. On this particular day, I knew that he had a major presentation to do the following morning and I was quite concerned by the level of the stress that it would cause him. He knew his material cold, but delivering it might be his undoing.

As a grade seven teacher, I have had the honour and privilege to attend many Bar Mitzvahs over the years. I noticed that not only did a boy become a man on the occasion of his being "called to the Torah", but that the practice leading up to his solo chanting recital at the Synagogue also transformed this boy for life. Having to face such a large audience, at such a tender age, was very intimidating, but the self-confidence gained from this experience became a lifelong asset.

So I thought to myself, if I can break down some of this boy's inhibitions today, maybe tomorrow's performance won't be so difficult. I walked down the row to where this lad was seated, and I popped up onto the top of the desk of the student beside him. I then sang "Mary had a Little Lamb", figuring that it is an easy song that almost everyone would know. The class laughed but most of the students were wondering what I was doing. I was known to do these crazy things for no particular reason, but what was I up to this time? My students were further puzzled (but no doubt happy for the break from schoolwork) as I had a series of them join me on their desks. Sometimes it was a trio, or duet, and even a few solo performances. At the appropriate moment, I had the student in question get up on his desk and perform as part of a duet, and then I had him repeat the song with me. Then I descended from the top of my desk, and had him sing it one more time on his own. When the period was over, I asked him to come and see me in my office.

"Do you know why I had you sing standing on your desk today?"

"I haven't the faintest idea," he said with a slight laugh.

"I know that you have a major presentation to make in front of the class tomorrow and I just felt that if you took some risks today, to the point of possibly making a slight fool of yourself, that standing in front of them tomorrow might be a lot easier," I explained.

The trick successfully boosted his self-confidence, and although he never found it easy to make presentations, that did not stop him from becoming one of the best actors in the LCC Players Productions. His stage presence was commanding and no one would have ever guessed that he was once scared of addressing large groups. Today he is a successful teacher in Vancouver and makes his living by speaking in public.

Speaking in public is a common phobia, and yet it is not often properly addressed in schools, which can be a detriment later in life to those afflicted by this fear. Fortunately this is not the case at LCC, and many years of debates and in-class presentations taught me and many of my peers how to write and to speak effectively ... two key ingredients leading to success in our chosen careers.

### Outside the Box

For many years, each member of the Social Studies Department had to take a turn recording and compiling the minutes of our 'cycle' meetings. I simply refused to do so and to this day I don't think my colleagues ever understood why, but it all boils down to the fact that I have trouble putting my thoughts down on paper – I never even followed the practice of writing out formal lesson plans. My mind is such that I sometimes forget my train of thought, and possibly some key points, while I am writing information down. Instead I have learned to use a small tape recorder when brainstorming in order to record my ideas for later transcription.

What was more difficult was finding a combination of teaching strategies that would allow me to reach all of my students, and I have always tried to reach them all. It is a seemingly impossible task, and certainly a challenge that plumbs the depths of a teacher's creativity. There is a way to "unlock" every student; you just have to have the patience and the determination to find the right key. In many cases, it will not happen with a traditional approach. To capture their imagination, you have first to gain their attention, and I found that doing something unorthodox, creative, or 'outside the box' often did the trick. You can't teach without their attention, so that was always my starting point.

Furthermore, you cannot teach your students if you do not convey the right attitude. I would enter my classroom with a smile and in a cheerful mood, as enthusiasm is infectious. If you are not upbeat, how can you expect your students to be? You have to set the example and students are very sensitive to their teacher's body language. I remember one morning having a most unpleasant conversation with a colleague, which put me in a bad mood just as my day was beginning. I tried to forget the incident and walk into my class in a positive frame of mind as per usual, and thought that I had succeeded. After second period, I went to my office for the recess break. There was a knock on my door and one of my female students entered, partially closing the door behind her. She quietly moved towards the edge of my desk and fixing her eyes on mine, waited to speak until she was sure she had my undivided attention.

"What's troubling you today?" she said with a concerned look.

"What do you mean?" I asked.

"You are not your usual self, something is really bothering you."

As I have said, you can never fool the kids. They know.

Another strategy of mine was always to enter my classroom and move around the room making contact with my students. One of my favourite ploys was to use an old Beatnik routine from the 60's. Approaching a student, I would stretch out my right arm with my palm facing upwards, and pretending that I was "cool", call out "Skin, Baby." The student would then slap his or her hand on mine. As the palm of their hand approached mine, I would quickly place my left hand on the back of their hand and say: "Ta" (Thanks). It was such a simple thing to do, but the kids looked forward to it and it established an instant rapport at the beginning of a class. Sometimes I also did this at the end of class, or to congratulate a student for a correct answer. I did this for years and my students never got tired of it, sometimes even beating me to the punch and calling out "Skin, Baby" as I entered the room. Unorthodox, no question, but it worked.

Occasionally, I did weird routines while seated at my desk. One such routine, I believe, originated from a comedian's routine on *The Ed Sullivan Show*. If we had gone a few minutes in a somewhat mundane direction, I would suddenly pull out my top right-hand desk drawer and speak in a pseudo European accent to an imaginary person within. "Sol...right?" I would inquire, while quickly closing the drawer. In a flash, I would re-open the drawer and respond as the invisible character using a very deep, heavy voice: "Sol...right," I would then close the drawer quickly and repeat the whole process once more. It was a seemingly silly antic, but my students loved it and it helped me keep their focus.

Two other focus techniques were borrowed from Geoff Merrill. The first was designed to get an entire class into the act, not just an individual. When I had outlined something that I wanted my students to note, I would pause, make eye contact and ask: "Get It?" to which they would respond "Got it!" and I would then reply with a long drawn out "goooooda" (good). It may have been my line, but most often my students would join in with me.

It is also great to have a gimmick for those pesky substitute periods where you are teaching a subject in which you are less than proficient. That was certainly my case when I was called upon to cover a class in French. Enter the "Donkey Serenade".

To perform this piece, you must use the imperfect (*imparfait*) tense endings of *ais, ais, ait, ions, iez* and *aient*. Select two students to play the donkey. The first student assumes the role of the head of the donkey and places their hands on each side of their head to form the donkey's ears. The other student stands behind, holding the former at the waist. Starting with the third person plural (*aient*), you can create a rhythmic chant for the entire class to follow, with your "donkey" moving around the class, both students kicking their legs out sideways in unison and the head flapping the donkey's ears to the beat. When the class gets to the first person plural of '*ions*', if you listen closely, by stressing the '*i*' as an '*e*' sound and stretching out the '*ons*' you can actually hear the donkey's neigh, which is followed by a crowd-pleasing cheer of '*i*' … '*ez*'. The exercise can be repeated as often as you like, giving several students the chance to play the donkey. It made learning tense endings fun and, not surprisingly, the students never forgot them.

I used a similar role-playing technique when I was teaching the "Brain Capacity Chart" of Early Mankind. They are a truly dull set of numbers, but students were expected to know them. Together we created a wonderfully diverse assortment of characters with which to work. We had an ape, a gorilla, *Australopithecus*, "Lucy", "Peking Man", "Java Man", a Neanderthal and, last but not least, Modern Man. For homework, I asked my students to use their imagination to play each of the characters for ten seconds, and then state their respective numerical brain capacities. I gave them a week to practice with the promise of a reward should their role-playing antics result in a phone call to yours truly from their parents. To my delight I actually received a few calls, as it confirmed that those students were in fact "doing their homework". At the end of the week, I would start my history class by having several students volunteer to perform any one of the characters for the enjoyment of their peers, occasionally asking a student to perform a specific role. I was left dumbfounded one day when one particular young lady responded to my request by saying: "Sir, I don't do gorillas!"

The first year I employed this technique, I had only one of my four classes take part, while the other three classes were expected to simply memorise the data. When it came to the final exam, almost all of those students who had to "perform" the chart achieved a perfect score on that section, while my other three classes scored much lower. With memory work, you have to find a way to make it fun and interesting, and whenever possible build in "reminders" for the students to associate with the data. You will achieve far greater results if you take it off the page and impart it into your students' imaginations!

I loved to play different characters and use accents. While I could do Scottish, English, Irish, and French accents reasonably well, my favourite bar none was "Newfie". As a student at Acadia, I had several friends who were from Newfoundland and over time I learned to mimic them at their worst. Sometimes I would teach part of an English lesson as a "Newf" translating back to English as I went along, which is necessary if you are unaccustomed to the accent.

Another favourite character was that of the buck-toothed Englishman. To achieve the right look, you wiped your top front teeth dry so that your upper lip stuck above them and you were off and running. There was one particular grammar class where I even surprised myself with the number of characters I portrayed and antics that I pulled. As I made my way out of the classroom for recess, one of my students stopped me and asked, "What are you on, Sir?" to which I replied: "Life, my boy, life!" However, I think an excess of caffeine on an empty stomach that morning may have been the real catalyst.

Whenever I had occasion to draw a map on my blackboard to outline some military positions, I could not resist eventually turning that map into a face. Using the particulars with which I was dealing, as well as some poetic licence, the face would slowly evolve and the key points that I want-ed my students to retain became key items on the face, making those points easier to remember. If art is not a possibility, curious or provocative statements also work. While in primary school, one of my own teachers used this numeric declaration to help us remember the length of a mile in feet. "At five, I went to school on two legs and I stayed there eighty years" (5280). I never forgot it, even though it is now almost obsolete in today's metric world.

### The Bell Hasn't Gone Yet!

While I was always looking for new ways to impress my students (in the hope that they would learn), there was one class in particular that left a lasting impression on me. It was a 7B class that I taught in the period immediately following lunch; these students had terrific ability and they adhered fastidiously to my suggested study skills. Their marks were outstanding: indeed they were almost too good, and I found myself having to defend their high class average to my department head, John Vlahogiannis. Much to my relief, he understood, indeed, he had faced the same dilemma on occasion himself. Sometimes, you have a class where everyone simply does well. As they were always on top of their workload, I had time to digress and have some interesting conversations with this group of young and extraordinarily eager minds. While we certainly went off the curriculum, it was still a learning experience, and they had certainly earned these unprecedented digressions.

One Thursday during that school year, I had neglected to put my watch back on following the games period before lunch. Following the meal, I became absorbed in a conversation in the Dining Room annex with a colleague, Ian Griffiths. Time passed, and suddenly I remembered that I had a history class during period six. I scurried up to my class, certain that I was very late; indeed, when I entered the room they were all sitting quietly awaiting my arrival. I acted as if I was on time and commenced teaching the class. Everything was proceeding normally, until twenty minutes later when my classroom door opened and a student arrived. "You're late!" I said. "No, Sir," the student replied. "The bell hasn't gone yet," and in that instant, the bell signalled the start of the period. With the exception of that one student the entire class had come early, and when I started to teach, not a single student protested or informed me that it was still their after-lunch free time. Just before the period was to end, I sent my one "late" student on an errand and suggested to the class that we try the same stunt the following week. It worked twice, until that lone 'tardy' student decided to start arriving to class early as well. As we regularly began our class twenty minutes before the bell, we invariably spent the last part of the class doing something interesting. It was such a treat to teach this unique class, where time knew no boundaries.

### Adrift in the Doldrums

I adored teaching my students and always thrilled in finding new ways to spur them on. Unfortunately, even the most fulfilling of careers will not necessarily fulfill every aspect of your life. As I approached forty and realized that my sporting days were behind me, I began to wonder if I myself had anything more to learn. This ennui was compounded by the fact that as one slows down; those dreaded pounds start to make their appearance, especially around one's middle. While I have had a voracious appetite all my life I was always able to keep my weight in line through many games of squash and hockey. But as my fitness regime slowed down, my weight gain sped up and over the course of the next six years, I gained considerable girth.

During that period, not only was I teaching a full course load but had also undertaken the role of Assistant Director of the Junior School. I considered this excellent training to one day perhaps become the next Director of the Junior School, but for whatever reason, when the position became available, I did not get the job. While it is an undeniable fact that life at times does not go your way, and can seem quite unfair, I had worked long and hard to earn that position and the feeling of rejection was difficult to hide. In hindsight, having gone through the process of not being selected and the hurt that ensued, I now realise that the secret to recovery is to step back, be objective, learn and move on. And so, the next year for me was, as Winston Churchill once aptly described it, "my wilderness year".

Something in my spirit had been wrenched and I desperately needed someone or something to re-establish my positive focus and get me back on track. As is often the case when one is going through rough times, a person or colleague (usually someone that you would least expect) will come into your life and bring about an enormous change to your mind, body and soul. This person was André Trudel, then Head of LCC's Modern Languages Department. André had been on staff for several years, and although our professional paths did not cross frequently, I liked him immensely. André had served in the Canadian Forces before becoming a teacher; he holds a Black Belt, Third Dan in Jujitsu and is a specialist in pressure point techniques. Furthermore, he regularly conducted clinics for policemen and had served as a body guard to Prime Minister Pierre Trudeau. He was, and always will be, a straight shooter, a character who, despite his gruff military manner, possesses extraordinary sensitivity. He was the man who came into my life at a crucial juncture and would totally transform it.

It was just after the Christmas holidays, when I and other members of staff found a note from André in our staffroom mailboxes. His note read something to the effect that we might consider coming out on Wednesday evenings from 7:00 to 9:00 p.m. for some calisthenics. It would help remove those holiday pounds, and at the same time we would have the opportunity learn some street-wise self-defence. I remember our first practice well. There were more than a dozen of us and I was without question the oldest by at least fifteen years. We walked into the Memorial Gymnasium where some blue gymnastic mats were formed into a square in the centre of the room. Sensei (teacher) Trudel waited for us there, barefoot in his white Jujitsu gi (martial arts uniform) and black Hakana skirt, accompanied by one of his martial arts students. It all looked so innocent to our group of complete novices.

Suddenly, André made his move and the student somersaulted high in the air and came down with a loud crash on the mats. Startled, I closed my eyes, covered my face and took about four steps backwards. I had come here for some good exercise and to get into shape, not to go flying through the air – a person could get killed doing things like that! As I began to plot a graceful exit, I noticed that all of my younger colleagues had also started moving backwards. The room was silent as we all stared wide-eyed and fearful at our instructor. It was a moment I wouldn't soon forget. The demonstration over, André stood in the centre of the mats with a big grin on his face. He beckoned us to come forward, which we did hesitatingly, while he stood completely still, looking back at us. Finally he broke the silence and said, "Don't worry, you don't do this until you are ready, and mark my words, some day you will actually enjoy it." At that exact moment, I don't think anyone believed him.

But we were to be proved wrong. Sensei Trudel was the perfect fit for my eventual success. He was intuitive about my abilities and motivation, pushing me as hard as any drill sergeant when I needed a kick in the butt, and giving the leeway I needed when my old bones were about to revolt.

His encouragement often came in subtle ways, but André never wanted to see you fail. The day of my green belt test, he asked me to do a lunging flip from a standing position, something I had never done before. I hesitated for a moment unsure how to proceed for fear of embarrassment or injury (or both). "Do you want to earn your belt today, or not?" sounded the stern voice of Sensei Trudel, and so I gathered up my courage and landed it successfully. Jujutsu and Sensei Trudel taught me that you have to continue to push yourself and, in my late forties, that was becoming an ever-increasing challenge. However, André never doubted my abilities or my potential success, and when your teacher truly believes in you unconditionally, you just can't let him, or yourself, down. This was a lesson that I took back with me to the classroom.

# Chapter Six
## *Non Nobis Solum*

I would not be writing this now if there had not been an actual, physical structure to house my stories. Without the School itself, there would be no memorable teachers, compelling anecdotes, unforgettable memories or an outstanding education for myself and those who came before and after me. Lower Canada College is owned and operated as a non-profit institution by its alumni. After even a brief time as a student, you realize that you are not just attending LCC, but that you, in fact, *are* LCC; it is your school from which to gain everything you can. Throughout its history, LCC has always attempted to provide every student with a solid preparation for life, teaching them not only facts and figures, but also important values and ethics. This belief is espoused by the teachers at LCC, and is a principle that is very much in line with the School's motto, "Not For Ourselves Alone" (*Non Nobis Solum*).

In the era before coeducation, a network of Old Boys' Associations (now Alumni Chapters), was established across North America and even as far away as London, England. Each chapter annually hosts an LCC Alumni Dinner or reception, and I have been privileged to attend several in a variety of cities. Furthermore, there has always been an Annual Alumni Dinner at the School, which until more recent years was a fairly low key event that was generally distanced from fundraising activities (or perhaps that is the grey hair speaking). The Memorial Gym served as the welcoming area and bar, and as a place for graduates to mingle. At the appropriate time, the assembled crowd would parade down the ramp through the senior locker room and into the Dining Room for dinner. There we sang the National Anthem, the School Song, toasted the School and listened to speeches from the representatives of the 25th and 50th anniversary classes. While there was some occasional bun-throwing by a few who had celebrated a little too heavily, for the most part these evenings were an opportunity to share old memories, renew friendships and rekindle the school spirit that lay dormant in all of us. And, of course, no dinner could be complete unless we were given the opportunity to stand and applaud the entrance of Chef de Grandpré and his staff with appreciation for another wonderful meal.

In the mid 1980's, Dave Wood was appointed as the School's first, full-time Director of Development. Dave is the personification of dedication and loyalty, and he is a passionate ambassador for the School, both as a coach and now as the Alumni Representative. I will never forget the time and effort Dave committed in response to each and every donation from an LCC Alumnus. His thank you notes were not form letters, but rather each was a personal handwritten response, often running several pages in length. Dave Wood served the School for forty-one years, and to me, he is the embodiment of the School's symbol: he is the heart of the Lion. Under his aegis, a solid base of operations for the Alumni Affairs Office of the future was established.

Sharing Dave's love of athletics was Trevor Smith, who joined the Staff in 1969 as a young member of the Physical Education department and over the course of his thirty-six year tenure proceeded to develop a truly first-class program of athletics. His motivation for promoting physical education is clearly evident in the following statement:

> "Physical activity was always one of the most important parts of my formative years. My fondest memories of high school relate to a wide variety of sports that I had the opportunity to play, and in which I enjoyed success. It was a very natural progression that led me to a career in physical education."

Under Trevor's painstaking guidance, the sports program was revamped. While football and hockey had been dominant at LCC throughout the 1950's and 60's, this was no longer the case. Soccer and basketball came out of the shadows and were considered equal – it was no longer assumed that the best athletes would automatically strap on some skates or toss a pigskin around. Individual sports such as golf and tennis were also heavily promoted, and the tennis team certainly received a boost by the presence of a certain star player who went on to an impressive professional career. Other sports such as cross-country running, curling and skiing were offered to those who liked to compete as a team as well as an individual. When I reflect back on the years from 1970 to 2005, I think that rugby has become one of the most popular of sports with the girls as well as the boys. If it is not the most popular, its players are certainly the most determined and enthusiastic.

I remember standing on the sidewalk outside the Webster Learning

Activity Center in 2001 with Trevor and a few other Staff members as the bus carrying the Senior Girls' rugby team was pulling in from a tournament at Bishop's College School. It had been a tough afternoon for the team, many of the girls were sporting black eyes, significant body bruises and three players came off the bus on crutches. As we watched them slowly make their way into the School, Trevor smiled that nervous smile indicating that he was expecting soon to be hearing from some upset parents complaining that rugby was too rough for their girls. The fact is that not a single parent ever complained; the girls were as tough as the boys.

### The Right Decision

LCC has undergone many changes in its first hundred years on Royal Avenue, and it will continue to evolve in the years ahead, but I believe that one of the most important events occurred in September of 1995. That was when LCC became a coeducational institution. This was not an easy decision and was undoubtedly a critical change in the history of the School. Of course it goes without saying that such a dramatic move could not have gone forward without formal approval from the members of the LCC Corporation.

This momentous decision was in the balance at a meeting held on June 7th, 1994, and attended by approximately 125 people, some of whom had flown in from across the country. It was held in the old Library, where the Heritage Wall, Social Studies classrooms and the Junior School library are presently situated. I attended the meeting as a member of the Corporation along with Paul Keyton, and it was a night that I will never forget. I believe that if the vote had occurred before the formal presentations had been made, coeducation would not have come about.

The Chairman of the Board of Governors, Dr. Paul Fournier, made a very clear and solid case for why the School needed to become co-educational. However strong the case was, the fact remained that the "old guard" were staunchly opposed to the idea of LCC becoming something other than an all-boys school. They were still focused on the past and were not aware of the challenges that LCC faced at the dawn of the 21st century.

That evening was a lesson in strategy and Dr. Fournier, master of strategy that he was, was up to the task. Even when verbally attacked, he kept his cool and avoided making the issue a personal one. Emotions ran high in that closed room as speaker after speaker made his case either for or against coeducation. Just when it looked like no consensus could be reached, potentially resulting in a stalemate, an esteemed old boy took the floor with the following remarks: "I have been sitting here all evening, and I have listened carefully and I have heard enough. Both sides on this issue believe that they are right, and both sides think that they have the best interests of the School at heart". There was almost unanimous agreement on this point. He went on to suggest that this issue was of such profound importance to the future of LCC that if we left the room divided, we would have failed our School. In the spirit of *Non Nobis Solum*, we had to stand united for the benefit of the School we all loved so much.

That was the turning point as gradually, even those who had been utterly opposed came around to the acceptance of coeducation. Members who had only minutes earlier been vilifying the idea now stood and demanded agreement for the cause. I remember the moment when Col. J.A. "Ding" Calder, one of the most senior of the alumni present and who had over the course of the evening spoken vehemently against the proposal, rose to his feet to propose our unanimous support for coeducation. A motion to that effect was immediately put to the vote and carried without dissent.

Eventually, all of the members of the Corporation present came to understand that their individual opinions were not as important as the long term success of the School. I am not sure just how many of the Old Boys know this, but when Dr. Fosbery incorporated LCC as a school for boys, he also included a proviso in the School's by-laws stating that one day in the future young ladies might also attend. While it did not happen during his lifetime, Dr. Fosbery had the foresight to know that there would be a day when young women would (and should!) make that walk up Royal Avenue.

Since the time when LCC first opened its doors, education and teaching have undergone enormous changes and are constantly evolving. Society was unequivocally patriarchal and it was assumed that women would only be a part of the workforce until they married. In other words, if a female teacher working in the public sector in Quebec in the 1930's and 40's got married, she had to resign her teaching position, as it was thought that she was taking a job from a man. My mother was just such a case in point. Once married, she could no longer work in the public school system, but, as LCC was (and still is) a private school and my great-uncle (Mr. Wansbrough) was headmaster she was able to find employment for a year – but she was one of the lucky ones. It seems like ancient history today, but how many people today realize that women did not have the vote in Quebec until 1949?

Of course, there were other contributing factors towards the shift to coeducation. Certainly, a determining factor inciting this change was the decline in applications for enrolment. Many of the families that had for generations sent their sons to LCC were moving out of province, often as their company's head office relocated to Toronto. Anxiety over the possibility of Quebec separating from Canada in the 1980's and 1990's served to move billions of dollars out of the province, and significantly decreased our pool of prospective students. Furthermore, Quebec law had decreed that unless at least one of a child's parents had been educated in the Quebec English education system, that child was obliged to attend a French school. This situation resulted in the untimely withdrawal of a few of our students and prevented others from enrolling.

As Assistant Director of the Junior School from 1985 to 1994, I had worked on the entrance procedures for grades five to seven with Paul Keyton. We would have as many as 150 applications for grade seven, and only about 30 openings. It was certainly a struggle as we realized that oftentimes candidates 31 through 60 (and even 61 through 150), whom we could not accept, were actually of a higher calibre than some students who had been admitted into earlier grades. However, the political unrest and resulting economic instability meant that our pool of applicants began to shrink, and it became harder to find students who were LCC material. There were still some quality candidates, but there were also some definite risks.

In all of the years that I organized and conducted entrance exams and interviews, I rejected only two candidates outright. When the second one of those students appeared in my classroom the next September, I marched down to the office and asked why my recommendation had not been followed, as I had in no uncertain terms indicated that this candidate would only be trouble. The answer I received was, "Do you want to get paid?" I think that was the day I became a staunch supporter of coeducation!

I have long maintained that it is not how many students you have, but rather how many students you shouldn't have, that will determine the success or failure of your homeroom dynamic. In other words, one rotten apple can spoil the whole crop. So if we were unable to attract a sufficient quantity of suitable male students, then it was time to find some suitable female students. At least, that was my reasoning, not to mention the potential benefits to our constituent families by allowing them to send both their sons and daughters to the same school. However, there was still one important factor: I had not as yet actually taught any girls, and had no idea what to expect!

As a grade seven teacher, I soon discovered many benefits to a mixed classroom. Boys and girls think differently and so bring unique perspectives to the subject at hand, which an experienced teacher can use to foster a better mutual understanding between the two genders. Furthermore I noticed that, while not a hard and fast rule, girls seem to have a slight academic edge on the boys at the grades seven and eight level, especially in their reading skills. This can be used to a teacher's advantage to tap into a boy's competitive nature and to push him to try harder.

Coeducation was integrated almost seamlessly at LCC because a majority of the staff wholeheartedly supported this important reform. It was not thrust upon on us to accept, but rather was something that almost every teacher and administrator had hoped would happen. Furthermore, the School was very fortunate to have the expertise and leadership of Edward "Ted" Staunton, who had become the School's fifth Headmaster upon the retirement of Geoff Merrill in 1989. At this critical juncture, Ted was brought in from outside by the Board of Governors after the two long tenures of Dr. Stephen Penton and Geoff Merrill respectively. Together they had run the School for nearly fifty years.

Upon his arrival, Ted Staunton was faced with the challenge of having to "reinvent" the School, as its operation had remained unchanged for half a century. It was a time of shifting attitudes, values, rules, parental demands and student expectations, and a new leader was required to be able to assess what changes needed to be made. Parents, in particular, desired greater access to information and a more meaningful involvement in the functioning of the School. What had worked in the 70's and 80's was not necessarily appropriate for the 90's, and the School had no choice but to change with the times. On top of all that, Ted also had the task of remodelling the role of Headmaster, shifting away from figurehead and mentor to a business leader role within the school.

Coeducation was Ted's ultimate contribution to the School, and his leadership skills and painstaking attention to detail helped to make it a relatively painless changeover. I believe it is the most significant shift that LCC has ever made, and it made my final decade on the staff an even more fulfilling experience.

Our fifth Headmaster also brought about changes to the School's infrastructure, as the guiding concept, as well as much of the planning and fund-raising for the Webster Learning Activity Centre, were undertaken during Ted's tenure. Ted was not with the School for the construction of the WLAC, which was built on the east side of Royal Avenue in 1999, but he was the prime force behind this new facility.

But it wasn't always business with Ted, for he had a human and theatrical side as well. Once during the month of May, a gentleman from England dropped by the School and asked to speak to the Headmaster. He was then summarily ushered into Ted's office, and encountered LCC's Headmaster attired as a Spanish matador. This gentleman had caught Ted on his way down to the Dining Room stage for the dress rehearsal of the up-coming Junior School musical, in which he had a cameo role. Surely all Headmasters dress in full matador regalia to receive visitors from overseas, don't they?

The gentleman was interested in student trips, so Ted suggested that he should speak to Mr. André Trudel, who was paged to come to the Headmaster's office. André was on his way to his martial arts dojo; hence he arrived dressed in his white gi and floor-length black Hakama, and sporting two intimidating black-handled silver scythes at his waist. After a short discussion, André intimated that Pierre Jean Tremblay was probably the best person with whom to speak, and the latter was immediately summoned in his "free dress" day apparel to Ted's office. There was a knock at the door and in rode Pierre Jean on his unicycle, blowing a whistle. He was dressed as a clown, in a multi-coloured shirt, wide black pants and sporting the traditional red nose – at this point I can only imagine the tales with which this gentleman must have regaled his pals at the pub upon his homecoming.

## A Change for the Better

In my last ten years of teaching, my homeroom was coeducational. While I really enjoyed the experience, it was definitely different from teaching only boys. I was careful to alternate, as equally as possible, both my questions to and answers from all of my students, as I always regarded girls and boys as equal partners in learning.

My attention to this partnership relationship was such a contrast to what my father had believed. My father loved my mother but, like many men of his generation, he did not regard women as equal partners. He was the 'provider' and the 'king of his castle', taking care to maintain the structural upkeep of the home (painting, repairs etc.) but he would not pitch in and help with everyday chores such as cooking and cleaning. These Old School values were most evident when my younger sister completed high school and my mother realized that there was no longer any point to her staying home all day. With her children grown, she was bored and wanted to go back to work. My father was adamant that she not do so. "You will make me look like I can't provide for my family, if you do" was my dad's retort.

This argument no longer holds much weight, as social mores and economic necessity have pushed many relationships onto a more even playing field. My wife Lyn was president of Creative Content at *Cirque du Soleil* for five years, and if she had held that position when our two children were young, I could have been a house-husband. A few years ago, she wanted me to consider giving up teaching in order for us to move to Las Vegas, whereas, if she were to work for the Cirque and pay taxes in the States, we would be better off financially than the two of us working in Montreal paying Canadian taxes. Thankfully she understood how much teaching meant to me, so she declined the move. How my father would have disapproved – "Your wife is working to support your family. That is unacceptable…out of the question!" – Oh how society has changed in the last two generations!

Although I embrace the notion of equality, it does not always have to be such a serious matter. And so, I developed an entertaining icebreaker for my coed classes so that the issue could be addressed with levity. I would have the boys in my class stand up, whereupon I would pause and make eye contact with them. Once I was sure I had their full attention, I would give them the following advice: "Gentlemen, if you want to have a happy relationship and a successful marriage with a member of the opposite sex, the solution is simple. Make her happy! If she's happy, then you'll be happy! But if she's not happy, your life will be miserable!" I would then ask the boys to sit down and repeat the process with the girls, giving them their own advice – "Ladies, the magic word for your happiness is shopping!"

I was never a teacher to withhold stories of misdeeds and mischief from my student days at LCC. Your credibility (or "street cred") certainly gets a boost if you can laugh at your own foibles and admit to having had your fair share of problems at school. The best approach I had found was complete honesty; I held nothing back and certainly had a student or group of students exclaim on more than one occasion, "Come on Sir! No one would actually do that!"

I have always believed that within the bounds of common sense and safety, rules are made to be bent, stretched or, on occasion, broken. During my student days, it was a way of proving myself to my peers – if you were prepared to take a risk, it earned you a level of respect and admiration. As my academic performance was questionable, it was a way for me to earn the respect of my classmates. And since I often broke the rules, I became very proficient at it.

As a student, one pet-peeve I had was being forced to do up the top button of my dress shirt. I have always had some difficulty breathing, and much prefer the freedom of leaving my top shirt button undone. I soon discovered that if I knotted my ties just so it would mask the unfastened top button. Even today, I never do up that top button, and as a teacher, this curious habit did one day come in handy.

There have been years at LCC when student attire did not always live up to what was expected. Many students wandered the halls and sat in their classrooms with their shirt collars undone and quite often School ties flew at half mast. There was little air conditioning at that time and the building was sometimes stiflingly hot and humid. While deep down I was somewhat sympathetic, I also felt an obligation to act in a manner consistent with my fellow colleagues who were attempting to remedy this sloppiness.

One hot afternoon I chastised a student for having his tie strung loosely around his neck with his shirt collar wide open, to which he replied: "I hate having my shirt done up!" At that moment I realized that I could offer a solution to this student that fell nicely between comfort and appearance. Using my two hands, I slowly pulled down the slip-knot to reveal my wide open shirt collar. His jaw fell in amazement. I quickly explained the technique: "The secret, young man, is in doing up your tie properly so that no one can see that your shirt button is undone. You didn't know my shirt button was open, did you? Have you ever noticed that my shirt was open at the collar…because it always is?" At which point I took the time to teach my students how to perfect this skill.

"However," I warned them, "if you are careless and don't have your knot pulled up correctly, other teachers will nail you for having your shirt button undone, so don't let them see that it is." Yes! I broke the rules and actually encouraged it. At least now almost all of my students were no longer overtly sloppy in their attire, at least with regards to their ties. I did this with many of my classes for years. It was a small, simple transgression, but I achieved the appearance the School wanted, while creating a special bond with my students. As a teacher, I may have been expected to set a good example, but I certainly was not going to do up my top button in order to do it!

In the spring of my final year, the Head Boy of LCC wrote an eloquent tribute to me, entitled "Sex! Please!", for the student newspaper. There is certainly a story behind this statement, which evolved from a random attention-seeking device to a well-worn catchphrase. I was teaching a grade 7 history period and had wanted to show some overhead projections. However my class was rather rowdy that day, and so as I was about to ask for the lights to be turned off, I instead called out "Sex! Please!" While I was merely intending to get my class's attention (and hopefully have them settle down) the boy nearest the light switch turned out the lights as if he had been commanded to do so. I repeated the phrase four times in a row, and each time the student turned the lights on, then off, then back on again. Finally, I turned to my class and asked "Does anyone here know why I had this poor fellow turn the lights on and off in succession?" The class just stared at me. "Well, as you are in grade 7, I felt that it was time that you realized that sex doesn't only happen in the dark." With the joke completed, I then turned to the boy and said: "Lights please" to which someone in the class responded "You mean Sex! Please!" This continued over the next few periods with this class, until I gave in and simply said "Sex! Please!" when I wanted the lights turned on or off. I didn't plan it; it just sort of happened. I was clear with my class that if anyone found this upsetting, demeaning or offensive, they should not be afraid to speak up, and I wouldn't do it again. However, no one objected. Did I cross the line? Maybe, but my students didn't think so, and that was what counted.

### For the Love of Fink

I have been very fortunate to have worked with many great teachers and students over the years, but one whom I hold in particular regard is Victor Badian. Not only did he take me under his wing as a raw rookie, but over the years we have become great friends. What I have always liked about Vic is his sense of judgment. Throughout my career, whenever I had a serious decision to make, or a difficult comment or letter to write, I always sought his opinion and he never steered me wrong. Right from the onset of my career, he became my mentor, role model and eventually, my best friend on the staff. He is the true embodiment of *Non Nobis Solum*. There are literally hundreds of examples of his dedication to the students, but here's the one that always comes to mind first. It was about 7:30 a.m. on a Saturday morning several years ago, and I was out for my daily run. It was bitterly cold and raining and as my regular route passes the School, I decided to stop in and retrieve an extra sweatshirt from my office. As it happened, Vic was to be honoured by the School that evening at the Lionfest dinner on the occasion of his upcoming retirement. Walking up to the front entrance, I noticed that Vic's car was parked outside and that the lights in his office were on. Curious, I bounded into the school and up to the doorway of his office.

Upon arrival, I inquired, "Vic, what are you doing here at this ungodly hour, especially on this of all days? Why are you not sleeping in and resting for tonight's event?"

Vic looked up from his desk and, in an almost apologetic tone, said, "Two Senior School students from the Lions' Senior Football team have a Saturday detention and won't be able to play in their game today. So I offered to have them serve their detention two hours earlier with me, so that they won't have to miss the game."

That was Victor Badian. Always there for his students, willing to go above and beyond the call of duty, even if it meant personal inconvenience for him. I once asked him what inspired him in education, to which he replied,

> "I guess my inspiration in education was seeing the enthusiasm for learning from the vast majority of the students that I have had the pleasure of teaching over the years, and actually witnessing the enjoyment those students seemed to

have in learning and being a part of the School. Their enthusiasm and positive approach made my thirty-seven years in the classroom such a pleasurable and rewarding experience. You could really feel that you were making a difference in the lives of young people."

I was so fortunate to have the friendship, wisdom and guidance of this totally dedicated educator from my first moment in a classroom to the last day that I taught.

Vic was a wealth of teaching information, and I often borrowed ideas from him, some of which I now wish I could claim as my own! One of my most valued tools was that of "Fink", an imaginary character whom I first encountered when I trained for three days with Vic in his classroom. He used "Fink" as someone who could never do what was being asked of him, and reached students in a way that a teacher could not. What a unique idea, I thought to myself and I took it upon myself to expand Vic's concept in totally new directions. Fink was invisible, a Robin Williams-type of off-the-wall character who captivated my students whenever he entered the room. I gave him an unmistakable high-pitched voice, and he usually made himself known to the kids with a silly giggle and a "Hi Guys!" During his visits, he would talk back, interrupt, contradict, correct me and even at times sneak up and attack me with his invisible hands. It's really quite difficult to actually script an interaction with Fink, as it was all ad-libbed, and for the most part Fink's dialogue was dependant on my audience's reaction. It just came naturally. However, a typical appearance of Fink might have gone something like this:

**Mr. Heward**: Today, students, we are going to study 'adjectives'. They are words used, in most cases, before the noun or pronoun they describe.
*(Enter the invisible Fink with his high-pitched voice and silly giggle)*
**Fink**: Hi Guys! *(Giggle)*
**Mr. Heward**: Fink, this is not a good time for you to be here. We are trying to learn about adjectives and your presence here will only be a distraction.
**Fink**: Adjectives ...adjectives ... what fun...what fun. *(Giggle)*
**Mr. Heward**: Enough Fink, please get out of my classroom now.

**Fink**: Ok! But you're such a meanie, Mr. Heward, such a spoil-sport. *(Giggle)*

*(Imaginary Fink storms off to sulk. Mr. Heward continues his lesson)*

**Mr. Heward**: Now as I was saying...

**Fink**: *(enters, stage left)* Hi Guys! I'm back. *(Loud giggle)*

**Mr. Heward**: I meant for you to leave for the entire period, not just ten seconds.

**Fink**: Fooled you! Fooled you! ... too bad ... too bad. *(Long giggle)*

**Mr. Heward**: Ok! Fink, if you want to stay, show me that you know something about adjectives.

**Fink**: To the ...jective ...to the ...jective.

**Mr. Heward**: What do you mean, Fink?

**Fink**: To the ...jective ...to the ...jective.

**Mr. Heward**: *(confused)* You mean the adjective, don't you Fink?

**Fink**: No!

**Mr. Heward**: Ah! Come on Fink, you're wasting my class time.

**Fink**: No way José! ...to the ...jective ...to the ...jective. *(Giggle)*

**Mr. Heward**: *(getting angry)* Explain yourself Fink or get out of my class.

**Fink**: Do I have to?

**Mr. Heward**: Yes, you do.

**Fink**: *(stalling)* Well.......

**Mr. Heward**: *(impatient)* Come on Fink, we are listening.

**Fink**: Well ......Mr. Heward. You said that an adjective describes a noun or pronoun.

**Mr. Heward**: Yes, So?

**Fink**: Well....... 'ad' in Latin means 'to the' ...to the ...jective ...to the ...jective.

**Mr. Heward**: You're not making any sense, Fink, you're wasting our time.

**Fink**: Sure I am. Right Guys? *(Giggle)* Follow along with me. Mr. Heward, you said that an adjective describes a noun or pronoun. So, kids, what nouns or pronouns are the most important in any sentence … you know … come on … the subjective and objective ones. Boring!... Mr. Heward refers to them as the subject and the object. Boring … boring… much more fun to call them …to the …jective … to the …jective. *(Giggle)*

**Mr. Heward**: I give up, Fink, you are confusing my students. Now get out of my class before I throw you out.

**Fink**: I told you that Mr. Heward is a meanie. Told you!... Told You! *(Giggle)*

**Mr. Heward**: Get out Fink!

**Fink**: Ok! But I'll be back. *(Giggle)*

*(Pause)*

**Fink**: Hi! Guys! I'm back and I found some more nouns to describe. *(Giggle)*

I was constantly improvising intelligent, yet amusing, dialogue on the fly, but Fink was always at his best during grammar periods. Playing the straight guy, I would pretend to be annoyed at Fink's constant interruptions and repeatedly try to banish him from my classroom, while making sure that the key points of grammar came from "Fink". The students did not always listen to me, but they always paid attention to what Fink had to say. He always made them sit up and focus and they could hardly wait for Fink to emerge. I didn't use him all the time, but when my class was working hard, or needed a pick-me-up, Fink would make an appearance. I felt sort of like the ventriloquist Edgar Bergen, except my "dummy" was invisible and could move around my classroom freely. Fink certainly ignited my students' imagination.

I have another anecdote that I cherish involving Victor Badian. And it certainly reflects his quick-thinking and ingenuity. For many years, a number of LCC Staff were involved in the annual Junior School musicals. During the 1970's LCC did not have its own stage, and we were forced to use church halls until we installed our all-too-small Dining Room stage in 1982. One year we mounted a production of *HMS Pinafore* in St. Columba's Church Hall, a few blocks west of School, and Vic was playing the role of the Admiral. During one performance, all of the lights in the church went out right in the middle of a scene. While it only lasted a minute, for those on stage (myself included) it seemed like an eternity. As

I frantically wracked my brain for a way to recover from this hiccup so we could carry on with the show, Vic, without missing a beat, had already marched himself up to the Captain, who was being played by Dave Wood. Without ever breaking character, he saluted Dave and said, "I'd like to compliment you, Captain, on guiding your ship through the eclipse." Gilbert and Sullivan couldn't have written it better themselves and we were off and running again.

And finally, Vic's dedication to the School was much like the school's determination to carry on no matter what. An example of LCC's singularity was its tenacity for staying open during fierce snowstorms when almost every other school in Montreal had closed. Shortly after one of these infamous storms, the Senior School had congregated in the Memorial Gym to listen to a distinguished guest and superb motivational speaker, Mark Scharenbroch, give a lecture. After his presentation, which was well received by the students, he was presented with a gift by the President of the Student Council. Mr. Scharenbroch, upon noticing the School Crest, asked the Student Council President for the meaning of the School's motto *Non Nobis Solum*. The student paused, turned and looked directly at Vic Badian, and replied to Mark Scharenbroch: "We never close!" I don't recall the entire student body and Staff ever laughing so hard. Even Vic blushed with embarrassment…or was it pride?

*Androcles and the Lion, 1986 (Andrew Tittler '87 at left and myself at right)*

*Tea towel classroom decor, early 80's*

*Before the crawl at Cheddar Gorge, UK*

*Tide commercial in the making at Cheddar Gorge*

*With colleagues Justin Guay '99 and André Trudel*

*Jujitsu, the gentle art*

*with black belt student Costa Ragas '01*

*2001 UK student trip, with Rick Barrett*

*Last UK trip, 2003 – Cheryl, Ian, myself and Vic*

*Prime Minister's Awards for Teaching Excellence 1999-2000,*
*(with Paul Bennett and MP Marlene Jennings)*

*All Blacks alumni tournament champions, 2005*

*40th reunion, Class of 1963*

*History Night Tug of War, 2003*

*History Night, 2003*

# Chapter Seven
# Forever Etched

### Little Did They Know

The stories I have collected over twenty-two trips to the British Isles with my students could easily fill up their own book. Each and every trip had its own unexpected moments and events, and over the years I began to look forward to when things would go a little pear-shaped (as they say across the pond).

In the summer of 1977, my wife and I travelled to the British Isles for our belated honeymoon. While visiting the quaint town of Salisbury, we discovered a spectacular climb inside the walls that ran above the nave of the cathedral, and then on upwards to the base of the spire some three hundred feet from the ground.

If you have read Edward Rutherfurd's novel *Sarum* in which he describes in minute detail the construction of this famous building, providing a virtual tour for the reader on the printed page, then you have already made that breathtaking climb. The narrow winding staircase ascends up from the floor of the cathedral to the top of the arcade (the first of three levels of the cathedral), winding ever higher as the enclosure becomes ever smaller. By the time we exited from this spiral staircase to the passageway that runs above the aisle towards the West Front of the Cathedral, I was already winded, but there were still two long ascents ahead of us. While the third staircase is a modern wooden construction, you still find yourself climbing eighty feet completely exposed to the world around you, protected only by a railing running along each side.

As I made my way up the staircase, I could see Sir Christopher Wren's reinforcing iron works, which were incorporated into the stone tower over two hundred years ago. The heavy oak planks onto which the staircase exits have been there since the 13th century. As I put my weight on them, I prayed that the builders had constructed for eternity! From there I took another tiny spiral staircase upwards within the walls, only to be faced with a nasty little vertical climb of about twelve feet. Ah, but this time there was no staircase. I had to ascend using iron rungs that were embedded into the stone wall (In recent years, a modern staircase has been built to circumvent the use of these rungs. It is great for the many tourists that visit the cathedral, but it has diminished somewhat the previously more "primitive" ambiance of the climb). The last rung was not on the vertical wall, but was about twenty inches removed from the wall on the floor of an undersized horizontal passageway which opens out onto a narrow ledge outside the base of the spire.

The view is spectacular, and you can look in all directions from the four sides of the base of the spire. Spectacular, that is, if you like heights. You see, I have a morbid fear when I am off solid ground. As I stood there with my heart pounding, the outside ledge rapidly filled up with other visitors and I found myself surrounded by a crush of people. A little girl next to me leaned through the opening between the stone parapets. In my mind's eye I imagined a strong gust of wind carrying her away to her death on the ground nearly three hundred feet below. I felt queasy and I leaned back against the stone wall of the spire for support; my knees gave way and I slumped down to the stone ledge. Suddenly, I heard our guide calling out: "Is that gentleman all right?" Seeking relief, I crawled on my hands and knees through a small wooden door into the safe haven at the base of the spire.

What a relief? What a view! I looked up within my little haven and could see the original wooden scaffolding erected to support the workers as they constructed the cone of the spire. A series of long wooden ladders and platforms extend upwards for approximately eighty feet, never touching the stone walls built around them. Beside me was the original round wooden windlass used to haul up supplies from the floor of the cathedral and amazingly, it was still in perfect working order. The tour left me awestruck, but I realized then and there that if I wanted to share this experience with my students I would have to learn to hide my fear of heights.

To this day, I am still terrified of heights, but I force myself to climb. As a teacher and one of the group leaders, I not only had to make the climb, I had to lead it. My solution on every trip was to seek out those students who had a fear of heights, and there were always a few. If they were afraid it meant that I couldn't be, and I simply had to pretend that there was nothing to be alarmed about. I would comfort them by saying "Don't worry, come with me and I promise to get you to the top and back down safely," and it worked every time. Little did they know that I was twice as afraid as they were, but if I showed any sign of fear they would never have made the climb, and the experience is phenomenal. The medieval building techniques and architecture that can be seen as you make your way up the spire are unforgettable, not to mention the view from the top. Ah, but it is such a long way down!

As phenomenal as the cathedral climb is, I think the all-time favourite activity I undertook with my students on those trips was the cave crawl at Cheddar Gorge. Each group of eight students plus their teacher and guide spent ninety minutes squeezing through minute passages, crawling over rocks covered in wet mud and wading through puddles of dank water several inches deep. Fortunately we were well kitted for the ordeal, as the spelunking company provided full-body coveralls and rubber boots for the occasion. Each participant wore a hard hat with a miner's lamp attached to the front; a long cord ran from the back of the helmet to a large battery pack worn at the small of the back. One could easily have made a Tide commercial, with before and after pictures of each group of crawlers.

While it was a fun expedition, I also appreciated the fact that the cave crawl was very much an exercise in team-building and, in particular, learning to rely on your peers. Each student had several responsibilities. The first one down the long slippery metal ladder to the Bolder Chamber had to call out the rungs remaining as the next individual descended to the tiny wooden platform at the bottom. Once there, each student took his or her turn. At another point, each student had to scale a small rock face to a ledge above using only their body strength and a knotted rope. The stronger students lent a hand (literally!) by giving a needed boost at the bottom, and someone was at the top to offer a firm grasp and a much appreciated pull up to the safety of the ledge. On two occasions during the crawl, each individual was attached to a safety line. The first time comes with the descent into the Bolder Chamber, which is fairly straightforward, but the second line was used for a heart-pounding, army-style crawl across a horizontal metal ladder that runs between two ledges high up in another chamber. The ladder was approximately eight feet long, narrow and spanned a forty foot drop to the jagged rocks below. The space between the rungs seemed to get farther apart as you inched your way across.

Once across, each boy or girl had to crawl along a narrow muddy shelf to a small opening. What made it difficult was that the shelf was not level, but rather it sloped downward toward the cavern floor far below. It was slimy and slippery and you always had that horrible feeling that you were about to roll off. To prevent yourself from actually rolling and stabilize your centre of gravity, you had to spread your arms and legs to your sides in an 'x', all the while making sure that you were allowing yourself enough slack on the safety wire to be able to disconnect from it when you made it to relative safety on the other side. Due to one's instinctual fear of falling, combined with the low-hanging overhead rocks that made up the ceiling, you tended to move along squeezed too tightly against the wall, which left you almost no slack whatsoever. Each person in turn had to relax and backtrack sufficiently in order to unclip their carabiner. Once there, you still had to crawl through a small aperture which was not designed for individuals as large as I was. On my early expeditions I would often get stuck and would then have to laboriously squeeze my way through, inch by inch, much to the delight of my students who were are already safely on the other side. One of the silver linings of my developing Type II Diabetes is that I was forced to lose 50 pounds, and from then on those small tunnels and openings were not quite as daunting as they once were. See, there is almost always a positive side to any situation.

I led my students through the cave crawl experience for nearly twenty years, but I will never forget my first trip where I encountered "The April Fool". We descended along a long narrow passageway where the rock walls converged into a large 'V' before us. As we moved along, the walls rose higher and higher and the 'V' compressed down to about half of its normal width. At the end of the passageway was a drop between the rocks of about ten feet, and at the very bottom was an extremely small opening through which you had to pass in order to get to the next chamber, known as "The April Fool". The smaller boys managed it well and thankfully mopped up much of the muddy water lying in the rock indentations within.

The only way to enter this geologic conundrum was to put both of your outstretched arms in front of you with your legs out straight against the rock face at about a forty-five degree angle above your head. It was like stopping dead in the middle of a cartwheel. Using the palms of your hands, you wormed your way forward through the small hole, ducking your head and shoulders under the protruding rock. I felt like I was trying to crawl through a U-joint under a kitchen sink. I slithered like a snake down the slope, trying to position myself to emerge up the other side, which I thought was within my reach. It was unfortunately at that very moment that my battery pack caught on the uneven rock above my back and I found myself with very little manoeuvrability, compounded by the fact that my arms were locked straight in front of me. I was stuck! You know that feeling …you have ten seconds to free yourself or all your back muscles revolt and go into spasm. Miraculously, I somehow managed to twist and pull myself free.

### Caught Undressed in the Upper Circle

On one of our early trips to London, Dora Parsons and I booked tickets for a play called *The Murderers*. While we had been able to preview the other five plays to which we were taking our students, we were unable to get much information on this one. What we did know was that it had been written by the author of *Sleuth*, Anthony Schaffer, and we reasoned that it was probably a good bet.

There we were, all twenty-five of us, seated in two rows of the Upper Circle with Dora at the end of one row and myself at the other end. The basic plot revolved around the central character wanting to murder his wife. Unbeknownst to the audience was the fact that he had a bizarre hobby of re-enacting murders, and that there was a nosy female neighbour who was always spying on him. His plan was to re-create the murder using his girlfriend as a stand-in (who would not be harmed) so that the neighbour would call the police. Upon their arrival they would then discover this gentleman's unique pastime, so that when he really killed his wife, the police would not believe the neighbour's report.

There we are, sitting in the theatre, ready for the play to begin. Early in the first scene, a tall, stunningly beautiful red-headed woman enters the living room and sits down in the middle of the davenport with her back to the audience. The central figure quietly enters and sneaks along ever so softly until he is standing behind her and, placing his two hands around her neck, strangles her to death (or so the audience supposes). He then bends her forward and we hear the sound of the zipper of her bodysuit being undone. There she is, naked from the waist up. Boy, you should have seen all the boys quietly slipping in their ten-pence coins to rent the theatre's opera glasses! Then with a quick movement, he strips off the rest of her clothing and she is stark naked.

A few moments later, there was a tug on my right arm and the student seated next to me said, "Mrs. Parsons wants to know if you think we should take the boys out?" I replied, "Tell Mrs. Parsons that it is a bit late for that." There was nothing to do but ride out the play. As we exited the theatre after the show, one of my sixth-grade charges turned to me and said, "You know Sir, there was a lot of nudity in the play, but it wasn't dirty." He was quite right. It was quite an observation from such a young man, and I have never forgotten his astute insight.

### "I actually heard that, Sir!"

On another one of our trips in the late 1970's, we had a student with us who was almost totally deaf, but could read lips very well. In the classroom, I had a habit of moving around quite a bit when I was teaching and in order for this boy to be able to follow the lesson, I had to be standing directly in front of him. I told him just to get out of his seat and come and tap me on the arm or shoulder when I moved out of his line of vision. I will never forget his smiling face as he ever so politely urged me to move back where he could read my lips. He was an amazing student who not only spoke English well, but even learned to speak French.

He really wanted to come to England with us. However, we were a little concerned, for a variety of reasons, one of them being that the traffic circulates on the opposite side of the road. In an emergency, his instincts would be the exact opposite of what they should be, and we could not use our voices to warn him of any impending danger. However, his parents convinced us that he could look after himself, and with a few special measures, we were on our way.

During our travels we attended a play called *Deathtrap* and we were once again seated in the Upper Circle. If you know the play or have seen the film, you will recall that there is a scene that takes place during an incredible thunderstorm. The sound effects were directly behind us, and the noise was so loud that it was painful. I covered my ears and did the best I could to block out the rude claps of thunder. It was really too loud! When the play was over and we were standing outside the theatre, the young student in question came over to me with a wide grin spread across his face. He looked at me and exclaimed, "I actually heard that tonight, Sir!" I was very happy for him, even if my ears were still ringing from the ordeal. He reminded me how we take our senses for granted.

### Terror in the Tunnel

Another memorable event occurred in Wales. We were six hundred feet underground in a former coal mine. It had closed in recent years, and now some retired miners conducted tours through certain parts of the mine. Our contingent had been divided into three groups, with a miner and a teacher accompanying each group. On this trip Mr. Gordon White, LCC's long-time music teacher, was with us, all six-feet-five-inches-plus of him. The tunnel shafts are not high, ranging from four to five feet in most places. I found it tough, and I am less than six feet. My heart went out to Gordon who for ninety minutes had to hunch over, but he persevered and survived it. Of course the students loved the miners' stories and scurrying around in the various tunnels. It was their kind of thing.

The rules were simple: be well-behaved and always follow your miner. However, one group was too excited and didn't listen. I was standing with my group, when suddenly, from an adjacent tunnel, out came four students running full tilt and screaming at the top of their lungs. They bore an expression of genuine fear on their faces.

"What's wrong?" I asked.

"There's a ghost in the tunnel," they stammered, pointing down the tunnel.

"What are you talking about?" I said.

"The eyes! The eyes!" said the boys in unison. "We were walking down the tunnel when suddenly we saw these great big eyes coming towards us."

At that very moment, a miner emerged from the tunnel leading a very old and tired pit pony. It did have big eyes, but it wasn't a ghost. It's amazing what dim lighting and a little imagination run amok in strange surroundings can do. "I suggest that you let the miner lead from now on," I said. In agreement, the boys capitulated, "Yes, Sir."

### The Royal Touch

Dora Parsons and I also organized one adult tour. It was particularly memorable because Dora had arranged for a special audience with Queen Elizabeth, the Queen Mother, and Princess Margaret at the Royal Lodge at Windsor. On the day of our departure, Montreal along with much of

Eastern Canada and the U.S. was firmly in the grip of a severe ice storm. When we got to Dorval Airport, we were told to go home, that nothing was flying overseas from Montreal that afternoon. Frazzled but nonetheless determined, I got on the phone with our travel agent, who miraculously managed to squeeze all twenty-eight of us onto a small plane which was to land shortly and then almost immediately return to Detroit. Once there we hoped to get on the British Airways flight that was flying directly from Detroit to Heathrow, avoiding Toronto, Montreal and the ice storm altogether.

Our party consisted of twenty-five women and three men. Dora and I had duly warned the ladies at our pre-trip meeting to come dressed in the appropriate clothing, as you were not permitted to meet the Queen Mother in slacks. Our original schedule would have allowed us to arrive at Heathrow, to transfer to our London hotel and then to proceed to Windsor. However, our circuitous route to London left us no time to change, as we were now going straight from the airport to the Royal Lodge, and many of the ladies had not worn the proper attire on the plane. Our coach had gigantic windows on both sides and upon noticing the gaping stares of the occupants of buses on either side of ours, I turned around in my front row seat to witness nearly all twenty-five women in varying states of undress, hastily making themselves ready for their Royal audience. What a ridiculously memorable sight!

The Queen Mother always did her homework. She read each visitor's dossier ahead of time and could remember almost everything that was recorded there. Naturally, the ladies were presented first with Paul Keyton, Chef Dick de Grandpré and me bringing up the rear. Dick was, and still is, a very passionate French Canadian and proudly Québecois. When his name was announced to the Queen Mother, she immediately spoke to him in eloquent French, and she knew all about his time as Chef. There were tears of pride and joy in his eyes afterwards when he recounted to me that Her Majesty had spoken to him only in French. It was an afternoon I will never forget. We were treated as long lost friends, with the Queen Mother and Princess Margaret putting on no formal airs.

Those British Isles trips, with their moments of uncertainty, were a labour of love. But, they were also educational and a great deal of fun, a constructive learning experience for all participants. The last trip I ran was perhaps the most successful but it was also the most difficult, as the

American invasion of Iraq commenced the night after we had left Montreal. Certainly safety was at the forefront of everyone's mind, but Bill Moger, our British coach driver of twenty-five years had the best outlook on the situation at hand: "Believe it or not, you are safer on this trip than when the IRA was active." It certainly never hurts to put things in perspective, no matter how daunting or scary they may seem.

## Chapter Eight
# The Best Prophet of the Future is the Past

*Most depressing was the way history was taught. I was not lucky enough in either high school or college to have a teacher who seemed willing, or perhaps able, to portray the conflict of fascinating personalities that underlies nearly all the critical moments of human experience. Reducing this great drama to the rote names, dates and places ought to be treated as a punishable crime. Let the tens of thousands of students who get their diplomas thinking that history was the dullest subject of their high school years be called as witnesses as we put the offending teachers in the dock.*
— Walter Cronkite, *A Reporter's Life*

Not all careers provide you with an impressive job or put a million dollars in your pocket. With that in mind, I devoted a lifetime to teaching history in a manner that made it relevant no matter what profession my students would later choose. My philosophy was, and always will be, that the study of history should cultivate the mind and broaden your perception and understanding of the world around you.

History helps to mould character and can have a profound influence on our lives; it teaches us that everyone has the potential to make a difference in this world. The story of Alfred Noble is a case in point. When his brother Ludvig died in 1888, a French newspaper mistook him for Alfred and reported: "The Merchant of Death is dead!" This is certainly not the way Alfred Nobel, the inventor of dynamite, wanted to be remembered. The event changed his entire outlook on life, and historians surmise that it was this obituary that influenced him to donate his immense fortune as a reward for outstanding scientific research and leadership that would bring both peace and advancement to the world.

No one can possess all the facts, but the study of history shows you how to see some of the *warning* signs of what could come to pass again. In a similar vein, my great friend, classmate and former CFO of a billion-dollar corporation, Geoff Southwood, believes that history is very important in the study of stock-market behaviour. As he points out, naïve stockbrokers will disregard market trends that have occurred and boldly state, "This time, it's different!" only to have history repeat itself in inopportune ways. If we learn to recognize and read these signs, perhaps unfortunate situations could be avoided. To improve the future, we need to study the past. The lessons of history are all around us and they teach us so much about humankind and how we can learn to live harmoniously.

Shortly after the film *Dead Poets Society* was released in 1989, I attended a couple of LCC reunions. Several of my former students approached me and asked if I had seen the film. I responded that I had, but why the interest? "You were that teacher." They exclaimed! "What do you mean?" I asked, and then I remembered.

In the mid 1980's, I had chosen a new textbook, *The British Epic*, for my British history course. As textbooks go, it was a good one with many illustrations, maps and interesting trivia. Yet on the day of my first class with my new students, I had wanted to impress upon them that one cannot learn history from a textbook alone. Before they entered my classroom, I placed a brand new copy of *The British Epic* on each desk. Once everyone was seated, I held up my copy for all to see, then climbed up on my chair and stepped onto my desk. My students, several of whom were new to LCC and thus not used to such antics, sat and stared in wide-eyed astonishment. Holding up my copy of the text, I declared that this was not a history book and then proceeded to explain why, outlining my frustration with history textbooks and the one-dimensional historical characters they portray. Historical characters are first and foremost human beings, with all the same strengths and weaknesses to which each of us is prone. Seldom does a history textbook truly bring an historical figure to life; more often than not it simply reiterates names, dates and events. And so, rant completed, I threw my book across the classroom where it landed with a loud clunk in the large grey garbage can by the door. I ordered each of my students to do likewise and the classroom erupted into joyful pandemonium as copies of *The British Epic* flew through the air into the now overflowing refuse bin.

What I really wanted to do in my teaching was to leave the textbook behind. Enter the wisdom of Paul Keyton. "What would you like to do if you had your own way?" asked Paul. "I want to throw away all the common tests and standard units, and instead study history through characterization." I replied. Paul listened as I outlined my ideas, and he ended the discussion by telling me to develop a course outline for his approval, outlining how I would then assess my students. With this I was given the freedom to teach relevant topics of interest to my students, with their main project being that they had to undertake an in-depth study of an historical individual on their own. At the end of the school year, each student had to come dressed as their character and submit to an hour-long interview, wherein they had to impress upon me what they had learned about this person as an individual and not just as an historical figure.

Recently, I had a conversation with a graduate of the class of '91, who made a point of telling me what an educational experience it had been for him to dress up as his character of choice, and to be given a full class period to present that individual's life and legacy. Moreover, he had found the question period at the end of his presentation was when he could truly play the role of his character. As a grade seven student, to be given the opportunity to not only perform but also teach his classmates was an experience that he attests he has never forgotten.

I have witnessed hundreds of outstanding character interviews, but the one I recollect best was from a student who portrayed Dr. David Livingstone. He was dressed to the nines, and came well armed with a series of large maps that outlined in great detail each of "his" (Livingstone's) journeys throughout Africa. He knew the man better than I did, and the interview went on for over two hours, as I was so engrossed in his presentation that I forgot the time. I had to apologize to him afterwards for the length of the session; it was just that good, and I was learning so much!

I wanted each of my students to realize that all historical characters were first and foremost regular human beings, just like the rest of us, possessing many of the same strengths and weaknesses. What made them historical figures were the choices they made. Certainly, wealth, background, opportunity and a certain amount of luck also played a large part in that person's achievements, but it still came down to the choices he or she made in life. What better way for a student to improve his or her own decision-making skills than by studying the choices made by someone who has made a significant difference in the world?

### Pinched Bottoms

History Night started with an idea and a $50 budget for materials, which we used to buy a large roll of brown paper. With the magic of paint and some ingenious taping, we transformed the LCC Dining Room into a medieval banquet hall. However, the heat from the crowded room and the candles on the table caused the tape to give way and considerable portions of the castle's walls tumbled down during the course of the evening, much to the delight of the students. We used to sit at tables that had been formed into squares with great sawdust pits in the center. Everything had to be eaten with your fingers, of course; no cutlery was permitted. When you were finished eating you could throw your Cornish hen's bones into the pit, although some flew across the room, an act that was repeated by many but had to be permitted as it was Headmaster Merrill who had thrown the first "bird".

Approximately two dozen mothers volunteered to dress up as medieval wenches to help out in the Dining Room. Alas! Several of the boys took advantage of this situation and some bottoms were pinched over the course of the evening. The 'wenches' were attractive and provocative and some of the boys just couldn't resist the temptation. In their defence, they claimed that their behaviour was truly in line with that of their chosen historical character. To be sure, in Henry VIII's case, it was!

One of my favourite moments occurred at one of the early History Nights, just after I was married in 1974. I was playing the role of Henry II in a scene from *Murder in the Cathedral*. I had really gotten into the role and, when in a drunken stupor, Henry II lost it with his Knights, I totally identified with the King. When I came off stage, I saw my young bride in the wings with a terrified expression. She was visibly shaken. "Don't ever get angry at me like that!" was all she could utter. However, we are fortunate enough to have hardly ever had a harsh word between us in 35 years of marriage. We occasionally think back to that play and laugh, but it wasn't so funny at the time for a new bride. Behold the power of performance!

Over the years, History Night has presented a variety of expositions. One of the most celebrated was a working model of the Great Fire of London, complete with lighting effects and a narrative based on Samuel Pepys' diary. We also had an RAF theme room, which housed the wooden frame of a three-quarter size Spitfire that was actually being built to fly.

There was also a cockpit with an aerial dogfight simulation, as well as a remarkable model of the coastal defences at Dover. With the planes in conflict and the aerodrome awaiting the call to action on the ground, it truly intensified the reality of the impending German invasion. In another theme room, there was an Elizabethan House in which leaded windows were etched with designs of that era. By looking through the largest window you could see a scene of 17th century London, with London Bridge as its focal point.

Naturally, the students' favourite theme room was our gigantic Torture Chamber which, by the time we disassembled it, had quite a sizeable collection of working exhibits and artefacts that had been eagerly made by willing Senior School student volunteers. The central machine was a ten-foot-high guillotine, which you had to endure lying on your back, facing the blade. The blade was only a rubber facsimile, but with a clever paint job, the dark lighting, and a little imagination, it looked real enough.

### Women in History Night (or, the Revenge of Widow Corney)

Even in the years when LCC was an all boys' school, I insisted that at least 15 to 20 of my students play female roles. How can you leave women out of history? The students were hesitant at the beginning, but I offered a ten percent bonus for those brave enough to don a frock, and led by example as I set the standard by courageously (or otherwise) portraying a woman in a School play. During the late 1970's LCC did not have many women on staff, and so when the female teacher who was to play Widow Corney in *Oliver* became ill, I was asked to take her place. I was not keen to dress up as a woman and appear on stage thusly attired in front of all the parents. The memory of my first rehearsal is still seared in my brain: when I had to cuddle up on the lap of my former teacher, coach and principal, Mr. Dave Wood, with a chorus of wide-eyed kids looking on. While I was well behaved in rehearsals, I was all over him when the lights came up at show time. And if the truth be told, he got me back by slipping straight gin into my glass.

I learned quickly that if you are a man and you are going to play the role of a woman, you might as well go all out. *Oliver* had a run of three nights, and the Widow had to sport a coat of garish red nail polish on her fingers for each performance. And so, I had a decision to make: was I to repaint my nails everyday or leave it on for my teaching duties in a prestigious all-boys school? I am certain that my actions mortified the more conservative faction of the LCC staff, while my supporters simply gave me a knowing smile and a reassuring tap on my back. "Go for it!" they would say.

Being a bit of an imp by nature, and spurred on by the annoyance of some of my colleagues, I just couldn't resist the temptation to have a little fun. At lunch hour, I walked to my local bank and purposefully sauntered up to the wicket of a new and unsuspecting teller. I stood there erect and touched the little pinkie of my right hand to my tongue and then drew it across my right eyebrow, all the while accompanied by some not so appropriate body language. Then with my left hand, I slowly slid a cheque toward this poor girl gently tapping my fingers daintily on top of it. Inch by inch my cheque made its way to the now horrified teller, who just starred at my fingers. In a mischievous voice I teased, "Could you please cash this cheque for me... (leaving a significant pause before I continued)... it's my wife's." The rest of the tellers all knew me to be a bit of a character, and thus were all smiles and chuckles at the obvious discomfort of their new colleague. As my wife, Lyn, has so often said, "Denys not only wore the nail polish, but he had to show it off." Thence forward it became almost fashionable to study and then portray a female historical character on History Night. I firmly believe that there is no such thing as dull history, only dull history teachers. It takes a little bit of personal eccentricity to give history the living colour it deserves.

### The Cockpit

It was my desire to transform my homeroom into something that did not have the appearance of an ordinary classroom that brought me in contact with Ian Griffiths, the School's senior art teacher. Ian's Art room became like a second home to me as I had always been inspired by what he was up to with his students. Over the years, Ian taught me how to do glass etching and stained glass. The stained glass panels that hung in my classroom infused the room with a cathedral-esque glow when the sun shone through them. These days I may well be retired, but I still put my skills to good use teaching glass etching to street kids at Dans La Rue, a local resource for the homeless and wayward youth of Montreal. As Ian has always said, "The best thing about being an artist is you can make something from nothing. It's magic, like alchemy. Nature is all the inspiration one needs to lead a good life".

In 1984, Ian and I scrounged the metal and materials needed to build a scale model of a Spitfire Cockpit, which was only four inches smaller than the real thing. This life-sized cockpit was a fixture in my classroom for many years. It was designed so that the student acting as the pilot could watch a small screen on which we projected footage of a World War II dogfight with the requisite soundtrack. While certainly primitive by today's standards, students could take turns sitting in the cockpit at the illuminated controls and experience the simulated aerial combat. The Spitfire was not only used in every History Night since its construction, but also as a reward when a student had made a significant improvement in his work or attitude, had done some outstanding kindness, or had achieved an exceptional score on his tests.

### Life is Good

Each year I would sit down with Rick Barrett, a great colleague and close personal friend, to write a series of historical skits for the characters selected in the upcoming History Night. What fun Rick and I had over the years. I remember the two of us trying to write a script for Bill Clinton, and realizing that what we had come up with was good, but was it *too good*? Rick chuckled and said to me, "If we use this material, where will we be teaching next year?"

We were not professional writers, but our aim was to present the most important aspects of a character's life in as entertaining a way as possible. Our goal was to show our subjects not only as the important people that they were, but also as human beings who had just as many foibles as the rest of us (sometimes more!). It was a labour of love but we enjoyed every minute of it. We started with the facts and then searched to find some personal touches that brought the character of choice to life. Over the years, we presented several pedagogical day conferences on the topic, "History Through Characterization". Rick even enlisted me to do a motivational address entitled *You Can Make a Difference* to the students of McGill's Faculty of Education. I remember this particular symposium well for many reasons, but mostly for the prank Rick wanted to pull on his friend, Professor John Bradley, who was running the entire conference.

Rick's idea was that he would go over and tell Professor Bradley that he had just managed to lose the super-expensive camcorder that had been lent to him.

"Rick! You can't do that. The man is trying to run this entire conference. He is up to his ears in details and stress. Don't do it, Rick." I said.

"But I really want to, Denys."

"No, Rick. You mustn't!"

"Oh, okay," said Rick, "but I really want to."

A few minutes later, I saw Rick chatting up Professor Bradley, and I just couldn't resist the impulse. I went over to the two of them, tapped Professor Bradley on the shoulder and said, "You know that camcorder you lent Rick? Well, it's lost." You should have seen Professor Bradley's face, but Rick's impish, uncontrolled, laughter gave it away.

Rick may have been a very conservative fellow but he had a marvellous sense of humour. In the thirteen years that I knew him we became brothers and kindred spirits. As I got closer to retirement, he used to kid me saying that he was going to take early retirement the year I left, as he did not want to teach at LCC when I was no longer there. Tragically, Rick died of a heart attack at the very end of the school year one year prior to my retirement. I lost my great friend and buddy and a piece of me would never again be the same.

There is no way that I can do justice to the many colleagues and student volunteers who have so generously striven in partnership with me to fulfill my cherished dream of bringing history to life. Over twenty-nine years of History Nights there were so many outstanding performances from students, staff members and alumni. When I think back on the hundreds, nay thousands, of roles that were presented over the span of nearly three decades, I cannot but marvel at the intensity given to each and every character and performance. My greatest pleasure was quite simply to sit back and enjoy the show.

I have already stated here that history is one of the most important subjects we learn in our formative years. I believe this not only because I am a history teacher, or that I wished to see all of my students become historians, but because it is through the study of history that we discover a great deal about ourselves as individuals, and about our collective humanity. If you want to bring history to life for your students, you have to make it relevant. Bring the past to the present. Use your personality and whatever attributes you possess to capture your students' imagination with stories, anecdotes and dramatizations. Play the part. Role-play. Recreate the situation. Bring the moment to life.

In 2007, this recently retired history teacher watched with interest the commemoration of the 90th Anniversary of Vimy Ridge as organised by the Government of Canada.. Some 5,000 Canadian students took on the roles of individuals who fought for Canada during World War I. Students from all across the country were involved in what was reported as quite possibly the largest student field trip ever undertaken. I could not help but smile with agreement and pleasure when I listened to the comments from some of these students as they were being interviewed on television. By studying and portraying a character, they saw history from a totally different perspective, and in many cases they had actually become passionate about the events and the characters they were portraying. I for one was not surprised.

One of my former students recently participated in the Vimy Foundation Summer Scholarship Program, travelling to Europe and visiting many military battle sites and cemeteries. Part of his preparation for this trip was to research the life of a soldier who had fallen on D Day during World War II. His name was Sgt. Albert George Smith, an only child who left behind a wife but no children. As my former student expressed it:

"I arrived at the cemetery and found his grave. While examining it, it occurred to me that he had left no one behind. His wife and parents, and all of his friends were in all likelihood gone as well. There was nothing left of this man in the world except a military gravestone and my knowledge of his existence. He had given everything that he had, including his future. So why do we remember? To answer that question we must look at ourselves. Every one of us has family, friends, hopes and aspirations, and so did every single one of the countless soldiers who died. They had everything in the world ahead of them, and they gave it all up for a cause that they believed in, a greater cause. There is so much more to war than just statistics. It is about the soldiers, the individuals. We remember so that all the soldiers like Sgt. Albert George Smith do not fade away into history, so that they do not become just a statistic. We owe them a debt for the freedoms that we enjoy today, and that is how we repay them."

I had nearly 2,700 students play a role during my twenty-nine History Nights, and nearly every one of those students remembers who they portrayed and how that person tried to make a difference in this world. The Vimy Ridge student involvement was simply History Night on a grander scale. It is something that each of those 5,000 students who participated will likely never forget. History was brought to life through characterization, and they had the glorious opportunity to live it. What better way is there to study history?

# Chapter Nine
## Moments to Ponder

In October of 1920, Dr. Charles Fosbery, the founder and sole owner of the School on Royal Avenue, announced his decision to give the School and its large property to the Old Boys upon his retirement. He did so because he was so moved by the involvement, genuine interest and generosity of his former graduates.

During the First World War, Dr. Fosbery communicated by letter with many of his former students serving overseas, sending them cigarettes and chocolates. They, in turn, sent him pictures of themselves in dress uniform, pictures which were displayed on the north wall of the Dining Room for decades. Following World War I, the Old Boys raised the capital to build the Memorial Gymnasium in honour of their classmates who had made the supreme sacrifice. The Memorial Gym stands as a testimony to the School's motto.

Each year on November 11th, this gym is host to a meaningful and often moving Remembrance Day service. The School no longer has a Cadet Corps, but it does invite those LCC Alumni and Staff who served during World War II, Korea and in Canada's modern military and peace-keeping forces. It is a solemn occasion, one that tries to make the act of remembrance relevant to the modern-day student who has not experienced the atrocities of war. Even as a retired teacher I return year after year for this service, as few organizations do it with more respect and dignity. The melancholy sound of a lone piper playing "The Last Post" and "Reveille" certainly stir the emotions.

A recent LCC student and recipient of the Vimy Foundation Scholarship stated it most appropriately when he said, "The truth is that Remembrance Day isn't simply a routine or tradition in which we are all forced to participate; it is in fact an honour, and a gift during which we choose to celebrate the sacrifices of this country's heroes."

While the Memorial Gymnasium has its own significance to the LCC family, it has also has also been witness to other significant moments in world history. It was there that I learned of President John F. Kennedy's assassination. The date of November 22nd, 1963 also happened to be that of "Speech Night", an annual custom whereby a distinguished speaker was invited to address the Senior School students and their parents. As we assembled in the gym that afternoon for a rehearsal, a wild rumour (from a student who had arrived to school after the lunch period) was circulating that an attempt had been made on the American president's life. The student who brought us the news had very few details to go on – certainly none of us believed that he had actually been killed. It was an afternoon I will never forget. We were lined up by class in the Memorial Gym with an aisle running up the middle. Our esteemed Headmaster Dr. Penton walked slowly up that centre aisle with his Bible tucked under his arm. As soon as we saw the Bible, we knew Kennedy was dead. Speech Night was cancelled; we were led in memorial prayers by Dr. Penton, dismissed, and sent home.

Up until that fateful day, the concept of assassination was not part of the political reality of North America, a fact that made President Kennedy's tragic shooting in Dallas even more unfathomable. I still vividly remember American news anchor Walter Cronkite fighting back tears as he formally announced the death of the President. During the week of events leading up to his state funeral, society was numbed by this overt act of violence.

That same feeling of shock and disbelief once again enveloped me on September 11th, 2001 in the wake of the attacks on the World Trade Centre in New York City. That morning, we were again in the Memorial Gym, this time for a Middle and Senior School assembly. Word came from a colleague, Mr. John Bower, that an airplane had just hit one of the Twin Towers and we thought that a horrific accident had occurred. However, when the second tower was hit, we knew it was no accident but rather a most heinous act of terrorism. I remember that day like it was yesterday. We were told to go back to our classrooms after recess and to carry on teaching in as normal a way as possible in an effort to keep our students calm. I had three straight history classes to teach, and for the first time in my life, I did not want to go back into the classroom. We teachers had assembled in the staffroom to witness a replay of the tragic events, and I was shaken to my very core – how was I to calm my students when I was barely composed myself? It was the realisation that we would only gain understanding by looking backwards, into history that kept me going. I went into each of these classes trying to calm my students' fears by listening to what they had to say and attempted to explain to them that what has happened in the past, or even what people think has happened in the past, affects the way we think and act today. If we don't learn from the lessons of history then mistakes will be repeated. The world has witnessed thousands of historical events, but it seems to me that too often they are just re-enactments on some age-old theme: my god versus your god!

## The World May Have Changed but the Basic Student Hasn't

We live in an age that is revolutionized not just by the forces of change but by the speed at which change now occurs. The first time I was ever on a plane was coming home from Acadia University at Christmas in my first year of college, and it was a plane with propellers! I didn't fly in a jet-propelled aircraft until I was twenty-five on a transatlantic flight to England. How many children today (LCC and beyond) have not flown several times to various corners of the globe by age ten or even younger? I began my life with street cars, no television, and the old gramophone record players, some of which you had to wind up! Compare these to what we have today, a mere half-century later.

Fifty years ago, the large majority of LCC's student population was Caucasian, middle-class and Protestant. This is no longer the case as the classrooms now reflect the multicultural composition of Canadian society. What a difference from when I attended the School! There were very few minorities, let alone visible minorities; for the most part the only difference was religion, as LCC had a small Catholic and even smaller Jewish population at the time. It was not something we questioned – it was just part of daily life. I remember Dr. Penton leading the entire student body over to St. Columba's Anglican Church at least four times a year for a supposedly "non-denominational" church service, which seemed very Anglican to me.

The world has changed and even the classrooms have evolved to the point where some are devoid of blackboards. The role of the teacher has changed to that of a resource person and facilitator rather than instructor. However, even with all of these changes, I am convinced that the child or student has remained essentially the same and still requires the same kind of support that has been traditionally given to them. They need to be nurtured, praised, encouraged to develop their strengths and to exercise their creativity. Most importantly students need to be taught to think "outside the box", question everything and develop a healthy curiosity about the world around them. Creativity expert Sir Ken Robinson has a lovely anecdote which illustrates the necessity and delight of creativity in the classroom. There was a young girl, age six, who usually sat in the back of the class for her drawing lesson. The teacher said that she didn't pay attention. "What are you drawing?" asked the teacher. "I'm drawing a picture of God." "But nobody really knows what God looks like," said the teacher. "They will in a minute!" responded the girl.

### Teaching and Nurturing Teachers

Each of the three Headmasters under whom I served directed the School according to his personal style. For the first twenty-two years of my career, Geoff Merrill was boss. He was a fun loving "Head" who seemed to run the School and keep abreast of all the comings and goings while seated in his large armchair in the staffroom. He was very conscious of staff morale and was very much a man's man, with a tremendous sense of loyalty to his faculty. If you made an error, he would always back you up publicly, while saving his reprimand for the privacy of his office. Make no mistake, you were held accountable in no uncertain terms, but it was a private affair. He only called for a full staff meeting when there was a reason to hold one, and very specific actions certainly took place as a result. He kept everything as uncomplicated as possible. "Let the teachers teach!" he would always say. He knew each teacher's abilities and expected you to devote your energies to your teaching and coaching. The staff under Geoff Merrill's tenure came together as a family, working side by side and socialising together, sharing educational ideas, methods and philosophies with one another. We interacted informally with each other, meeting "unofficially" whenever it was deemed necessary, and it culminated in our learning a lot from each other.

In my opinion, schools today have reduced this valuable method of informal discussion as an agent of learning and exchange in an attempt to streamline interaction to only occur in a formal setting. The idea behind this management approach may have merit, but I believe that educators may have lost much of what they had hoped to gain and a large amount of spontaneity and openness has been sacrificed.

In recent years, under the leadership of teachers Brian Moore and Steeve Lee, a number of LCC staff members convene once a month during the school year for an evening meeting over dinner to share and discuss any and all aspects of teaching and pedagogy. The group is called "Critical Friends" and is open to any and all Staff members. I recently attended one such meeting and was impressed by the diversity of the issues that were tabled for discussion, and by the honest way each member of the group responded to the evening's topics. There was a genuine effort made by each member to offer solutions to the problems that fellow teachers were encountering, and it was a truly worthwhile forum for exchange.

I have always had time for "good" meetings, and I only objected to those meetings that could have easily been replaced by a memo, as they were a waste of valuable time that could be spent more profitably with my students. My argument is really with the process, as I believe that too much of our energy as a teacher is being diverted away from teaching and towards dealing with administrative red tape. Call me old-fashioned, but I have always felt that the School's administrative bodies should deal with these concerns, and leave the teachers free to do what they do best, teach. This is certainly one of the most important changes in education that I have witnessed over the years.

Teaching is a very demanding profession and it takes a great deal of physical and emotional energy and stamina to be a good teacher. It also involves a tremendous time commitment, which is not always obvious to the outside observer. While it is true that teaching can be a profession where one just "goes through the motions", it is also a career to which you can dedicate all twenty-four hours of your day. Those who just go through the motions don't belong in the profession, and they seldom gain the respect of their students. One thing about students is that they cannot be fooled. They recognize the phonies and know which teachers are not committed to the job. Ask any conscientious group of students to identify the best teachers in any school, and their list will almost invariably be right on.

When I reflect back on my teaching career, I realize that the fact that I started off with no official training or experience was actually a blessing in disguise. I had to rely on my instincts and wits alone, and I had to work hard to find the answers to many essential questions:

What was it that made a student want to work harder
for certain teachers?
Why are students willing to take a "leap of faith" for

one teacher and yet resist another tenaciously?
What kind of teacher made me want to learn?
What teachers instilled in me a feeling of self-confidence and
self-worth?
What teachers showed me a sense of trust and respect?
What are the important attributes of an outstanding teacher?

Without knowing how to answer these questions, a teacher will more than likely find themselves up the proverbial creek without a paddle.

Teaching is a bit like scuba diving; when you dive under the surface, you are a visitor to another world. It is not your world; you are but a guest. When you teach, you enter the students' world of wonder to share in their discoveries, joys and dreams. As Sir Ken Robinson affirms: "Every student has academic talents but often what he or she is interested in at school isn't valued or is even stigmatized… They don't all sit still and listen. Some need to move to think." In the early 1960's, too many teachers and schools were overly concerned with conformity. As teachers, we should remember that students often learn best in their own way. We should be encouraging diversity of thought, and trying always to promote that most special of gifts: the gift of imagination.

I have always tried to take the positive approach. Find first what your student can do well, encourage and develop their ability and self-confidence, and then build from there. Good teachers are born to be teachers and instinctively know what to do to be effective. That is not to say that any teacher is perfect or can't improve his or her teaching skills. All of us need to continue learning and sharing our experiences, and the concept of conferences and well-planned pedagogical days is a good one (certainly we didn't have enough of them in my early years of teaching). While I usually found conferences to be excellent, many of the pedagogical days proved to be rather disappointing. If you are going to give up a teaching day for a pedagogical day, then do it right and be sure to do the required research. It is essential to spend money and do whatever is needed to address the School's diverse departmental concerns.

### Bon Cop, Bad Cop

Teachers at LCC have traditionally been called upon to do substitution duty from time to time. We didn't get any extra pay for this; it was something we just accepted as part of the job. I always looked on it as an opportunity to catch up with and enjoy students that I didn't see as frequently as others. Most 'subs' occur at the grade level at which a teacher is regularly teaching, thus the vast majority of my extra classes were at the Middle School level. However, on occasion when the School was really short-staffed, we would be called upon to cover the senior grades.

In my final year I was asked to cover a grade ten class for one of my colleagues with whom I had a great relationship. The teacher had warned me that the class was a bit of a wild bunch. I had taught them all in grade seven, and while they were indeed a handful, they were positive, well-meaning kids who just had an excess of energy that they were going to expend one way or another. My colleague had asked me to collect a major assignment that was due that day. Fearing that the students might try to use their usual teacher's absence as an excuse, I was warned that I would probably only receive a handful of them, but would I please do my best to round up as many assignments as possible.

I entered the classroom at the appointed hour and, to my amazement, was given a standing ovation by this group of former students. Maybe they were genuinely happy to have me as their substitute, but they were probably also hoping that I would be a pushover and allow them to have a free period. I was immediately struck with the idea that this was the perfect occasion to employ the standard "good cop, bad cop" routine. I scanned the class in front of me and announced that I had a real problem.

"I gather that you have a major assignment due for this period," at which point I quietly asked for a show of hands from students who had actually completed the work. Only a few hands were timidly raised. I sighed deeply and pretended to look worried as I proceeded to inform them that their teacher had stipulated that anyone not handing in their essay that period was to receive a Saturday morning detention. While I was certainly stretching the truth here, I had been asked to use whatever means necessary to collect those essays. I carried on with my ruse, saying "Look! I have taught all of you and I like you guys, and I really would feel badly having to bring any of you in on Saturday." They looked at me with a glimmer of hope in their eyes. "Listen," I said, "I am going to be at school until 7:00 p.m. tonight, maybe even later conducting some History Night rehearsals. If you are willing to stay after school and complete your assignment, and can get it to me before I leave, I'll simply put your project in my colleague's staffroom box with the others, and you can avoid the Saturday morning detention." Some managed to finish their work during the period while others stayed after school, and by seven o'clock that evening I had every one of their assignments on my desk.

On another occasion, I was asked to cover a grade 11 class. At the beginning of the period, only five students had arrived in class. I allowed a three minute grace period, and then as each successive student arrived, I informed them that they had to "hit the deck" and give me twenty-five push-ups on the spot. There were no exceptions for the girls, though they were allowed to do modified push-ups (from the knees instead of on their toes) and to position themselves so that they were not in a compromising position in their kilts. While dumfounded at the request, each latecomer performed the task without argument. After the last student had arrived and completed his penalty, one girl said to me, "You never made us do push-ups when we were in grade seven."

I smiled and replied, "But, you were never late for my class in grade seven."

## Chapter Ten
# A Final Walk Up Royal Avenue

### *Maternity Leave ... You have to be Kidding!*

In the late 1960's and 70's, approximately fifteen new faculty members joined LCC and many of them, like me, would teach their entire career at the School. It was thus that, at the end of my career, I witnessed an influx of new teachers who were hired to take the place of these retiring veterans, myself included. The School's new hiring practices also ensured a more equitable ratio of male-to-female teachers. Female teachers were few and far between in the past, but now they comprise half of the staff or more, particularly in the Junior School. One major sign of the changing times is the issue of parental leave benefits. Today, even husbands receive at least a week off with pay to attend to their wife and new child. What a difference! When my daughter Kelly was born in November of 1978, there was no such system in place for a first-time father such as myself to take some time to be with his newly hatched family. Fortunately, she was born on a Saturday, and so there was no conflict with my teaching duties. After all, I had Sunday to recover!

However, when my second child was born, my son Stephen, I did not have the luxury of a day off. He was scheduled to arrive on a Tuesday via C-section, which he did on the morning of September 16th, 1980. A policy allowing a male teacher to go to the hospital to participate in the birth of his child was not yet in place. I was fortunate to have the second period of the day as a spare, but other than that I had a full slate of classes. It was left to your colleagues to help you out, which is exactly what happened in my case. Long-time Junior School teacher Jim Dimock, a very thoughtful and decent fellow, offered to cover my third period class so that I could indeed attend the birth of my son; if I skipped lunch, it meant that I could be away from the school from 9:15 in the morning until 1:00 in the afternoon. That was just the way it was when I was a young teacher, and so I returned to school for my afternoon classes. Of course, now things have changed and it is far more likely that the exuberant father-to-be calls out as he bounds down the main steps, "See you in a week's time!"

My son's birth was complicated. But our physician, Dr. Edmund De-Koos, dealt with the problem quickly and decisively and delivered our son safe and sound. Needless to say, I was emotionally charged about Stephen's arrival and especially overjoyed at the excellence of our doctor. Upon my return for my afternoon classes I was understandably euphoric and eager to share this harrowing, but joyous, experience with my students. That evening at the hospital I ran into Dr. DeKoos who said, "I hear you said some wonderful things about me in your classroom this afternoon."

"As a matter of fact, I did, but how do you know?"

Dr. DeKoos explained that his nephew was in my homeroom. I hadn't the slightest idea. But I don't think I could have found a better way if I had tried to convey my heartfelt thanks to our doctor than in the way that it had played out.

### From Clunky Machines to Sophisticated Gadgets

The 1990's onward brought great change to education, but without doubt the most profound innovation in teaching today has been the introduction of technology into the classroom. There were no computers when I was a student or even when I began my teaching career. At report card time, we were permitted to use a massive metal adding machine, with an arm on its right side like a slot machine, to help compute our class averages. A simple calculator was unheard of, and when the first ones hit the market some years later they cost well over a hundred dollars (a huge sum of money in those days). I can remember fund-raising for the School's first computer in 1976-77. This was quickly increased to four, then twelve and finally twenty-eight, giving each student in a class the opportunity to make use of their own Apple computer in the School's lab, which was aptly dubbed "The Apple Orchard".

Around that time the School started some limited information technology (IT) training for its staff, and a group of us were assembled in front of a computer screen in the "Orchard" to begin our instruction. But we were not alone; we were sharing the lab with the School's "whiz kids", who seemed to operate these machines effortlessly as every keystroke worked miraculously for them. While duly impressed, we were also greatly intimidated by these boys. We pretended that we knew what we were doing, but in reality, we didn't have a clue. Finally one of these "wunderkinds" had seen enough. He wandered up to me discreetly and looked over my shoulder at my computing efforts. I looked up at him as if to say: "What?"

He bent down and spoke to me. "Would you like me to show you how to turn it on, Sir?"

"Yes, please." I said, "And while you're at it, would you like to pull up a chair and show me how it works?"

We reversed roles that afternoon; he was the teacher and I was the student. For the rest of my career, whenever my computer became an enigma to me, I simply turned to my class and said, "Help!" They never let me down, but they fixed my problems so easily and quickly that I could hardly follow what they had done.

Today's children pick up and play with computers the way we once amused ourselves with crayons or Lincoln Logs. It is second nature to them, and I am so envious. While I can perform the basic operations, I am by no means computer literate, but now, even I find it impossible to function without one.

My generation will recollect the film strips that had to be loaded manually, and which the teacher had to advance in the projector frame by frame, cued by the "beep" from the accompanying audio narration. We also had primitive slide projectors, in which a teacher had to insert a slide, backwards and upside down, one at a time through a horizontal mechanism.

And what about those large cumbersome, seemingly pre-historic "opaque" projectors, used mainly for enlargements? Clunky as these machines were, they did the job they were designed for. I remember using one with Ian Griffiths to enlarge certain images that we wanted to make into gigantic wall murals for History Night. Canvas, a supply of pencils, masking tape, an opaque projector and a gymnasium wall were all you needed. Oh, yes, and lots of time!

Whenever a film was needed for teaching duties, the 16mm print would have to be loaded onto the school's lone projector. Films had to be ordered in advance from the National Film Board of Canada (NFB), and the Audio Visual Auditorium (AVA) had to be reserved for that period. Calling the AV room an auditorium by today's criteria would be ludicrous, but that is how it was designated. When I think back on the old AVA, I have memories of dust, shelves of rock samples, drying paint applied to clay relief models and decaying film strips. And, not to be overlooked was the school's dark room, located in a closet with a dark-panelled door at the front of the classroom near the side wall containing several enormous windows. It was larger than most of the classrooms, with more rows of seats to fit students and, of course, home to all of that now antiquated technology. Even most of the tape recorders were reel-to-reel, and the sound was always played through some archaic speakers that should have been discarded years before. Stereo! You have got to be kidding!

In contrast, the LCC of today is one of the leading schools on the continent in the area of technology. In discussions with Gary Millward, who was responsible at the time for technology at LCC, I was astounded by the rapid growth in demand for technology at the School. In 1998, the budget for computers and technology was $24,000. In 2007, that same budget was 1.4 million dollars. If that doesn't say it all! The AVA budget in my day was probably $50 to buy a couple of replacement bulbs for the School's sundry machines.

Beyond computers, the School's current application of technology to the study of music is particularly impressive. Using the program Smartmusic, each student is able to practice his or her instrument of choice while a computer analyses the performance. Graphics produced by the computer indicate the mistakes, and it can even provide an evaluation score. With the program Finale Notepad, students can synthesize a piece of music that they have composed. With these programs, even a student with average musical ability is able to expand his or her repertoire to include composition, analysis, production, engineering and recording. Furthermore, the extensive recording studio provides the means for students to develop a more integrated appreciation and knowledge of music.

This type of technology would have really inspired me to learn. With my learning difficulties, I might not have had the skills to master an instrument, but I would potentially have been able to cultivate other musical aptitudes. After my experience in the music lab, I felt like I wanted to go back to grade seven and start all over. One cannot compare LCC's music program of today to that which came before, when singing was the main component with some recorder training and musical theory thrown in for good measure. Vive la différence!

Of course, technology can only take a student so far, and for all the technological leaps and bounds, LCC has not forgotten the human factor. Certainly self-directed learning is an important part of a student's education, but they cannot learn everything on their own, especially such skills as critical thinking. Hence, daily interaction with knowledgeable teachers remains at the core of the LCC learning experience.

### The Death of a Word

Although the teaching of history was my primary vocation, I also taught English, and for the last few years of my teaching career directed the grade eight drama program. English is such a broad subject to teach, as it has an abundant number of themes and ideas that a teacher can explore and develop. But English is not all fun and games as it also covers such mundane topics as grammar and punctuation. Each teacher has his or her own approach to dealing with such tedious topics, and I was always seeking devices to make them more engaging for my students.

One evening I sat watching a TV special starring the late Victor Borge, who was performing his famous punctuation routine in which he made a special sound effect for each punctuation mark. As I chuckled away at Borge's antics, I realized that this sketch was perfectly designed for the classroom. I had my students write a short passage in English in which they had to correctly use as many punctuation marks as possible. Using a ghetto blaster and a microphone, I then had them read out their passages, re-creating the corresponding sounds. For consistency and simplicity's sake, we stuck with the same sounds that Victor Borge had employed in his routine, but it was certainly hard to keep a straight face when practicing those sound effects as a class. Some students opted to conduct their classmates to make the appropriate sounds by gesturing with their hands, like a musical director with a baton. It gave the students the resolve to use each and every punctuation mark, and it was a genuinely amusing diversion.

Having graded essays for nearly three decades, I became somewhat vexed at how often my students used the word "nice" in their compositions. Even with well over 200,000 words in the English language, my students still seemed to think that "nice" was the best term for describing such things as an enjoyable event, a stunning photo or a genuine and caring individual. Drastic measures needed to be taken, and I resolved to kill off "nice" once and for all, thereby eradicating it from my students' vocabulary. I arrived at class one morning with a large shovel, a sheet of paper, a red pen and a plastic bag. I circulated the sheet of paper and pen around the class, instructing each of my students to write the word "nice" in red (signifying blood) for the last time in their lives. When every student had finished I sealed the sheet in the bag and then marched my students out of my classroom, down the stairs and out of the School. Outside, we solemnly formed a cortege and I informed my students that we were going to bury the offending word in the field. Some students broke spontaneously into a funeral dirge and, as I dug a hole, several Jewish students collected small rocks, as per custom, to place on the grave. Together we buried the word "nice", never to be used again. Sometimes unorthodox methods can have an unparalleled impact on your students.

The study of drama is marvellous for the creativity that lives within each student. From time to time we would play improvisational games like the ones that were used on the TV program *Whose Line Is It Anyway?* In fact, students would write many of the scenarios themselves. Drama class always brought about pleasant surprises and I was utterly caught off guard by one of my most intelligent and diligent students. She enjoyed drama class but was somewhat reserved and often seemed to hold herself back during exercises. We were playing a game in which a scenario would be given and each student had the option of coming up to the front of the stage and presenting a one-liner. The category was "Things you should never say to your mother", and the student in question ambled up to the front of the stage, paused, looked about mischievously and asked: "So, how was Dad last night?"

The intense generosity of spirit and creativity exhibited by my drama students made that subject one of my most memorable assignments. I certainly enjoyed watching my students do improv, but I also had them perform using existing material. As well as performing monologues by others, I would have my students write and perform original work. One hectic Friday morning a female student of mine meekly entered my office. She gently folded a sheet of paper and placed it on my desk, asking me to read it as soon as I could, and then left the office. I had intended to read it promptly, but it was one of those incredibly busy days, and so it got pushed to end of a long line of priorities.

"Have you read it yet?" she asked me in the lunch room.

"No, I haven't," I said, "I am sorry. It is just one of those days, but don't worry, I will!"

The day passed and I was just about to make my way home when I remembered her note. I figured that a few more minutes in the office would do me no harm, and she had seemed so keen for me to read it. I unfolded her neatly folded missive and as I began to read was completely shocked by its contents – her father had walked out on her mother for a much younger woman, shattering the family. I felt terrible and so helpless. This student had needed me, indeed she had come to me for help, and I had let her down. I knew the mother and father and was therefore surprised by these events as they seemed like such a loving couple. Although uncomfortable about this, worse was the nagging feeling that I had failed to be there for one of my students. I had a most unsettling weekend as this poor girl's plight was never far from my mind. Monday morning I rushed to school to catch up with her first thing, expecting to offer condolences and an apology. To my surprise, she had a wide smile on her face and rushed over to meet me, asking anxiously, "Did you read it? What was your reaction? Did you like my original monologue?"

There is rarely a dull moment when teaching drama, and it certainly provides you with more than its fair share of surprises. One of my profound joys was when my daughter Kelly, an accomplished performer in her own right, came to LCC and directed three Middle School productions: *Mission Possible, The Legend of Sleepy Hollow* and *Parlour Games*. And helping Kelly in her work was her capable assistant, that very same student whose missive had deprived me of sleep for an entire weekend!

## Every Day is a Gift

My great friend Rick Barrett, who taught grade six, was a staunch proponent of making the most of each and every day. Rick and I regularly dropped in on each other's classes for some tag-team teaching, and sometimes just kibitzed or told stories to each other's students. These visits were also an opportunity for me to get better acquainted with students I would be seeing in my class next year, and for Rick to walk down memory lane with his former students who were now in my grade seven class. Several years ago, Rick asked me to drop in on his grade four class to recount some stories about the history of LCC. That particular day is forever etched in my memory as my all-time favourite teaching experience. One story led to another, and my ten minute guest spot turned into a full period of tales and revelry. The kids were beside themselves with laughter and glee as Rick and I were at our best.

When the bell sounded to end the period, I exited the class and walked down the corridor to my office, pitying the poor teacher who would have to try and teach those kids next period. Unbeknownst to me, Rick was that unfortunate person as he had them for a double period. At the end of the school day, Rick entered the staffroom and saw me standing there. I could tell by his vexed expression that he had a tough ride for the last forty-five minutes. "I couldn't teach them anything," he bellowed, "You rascal! You had them all turned inside out with excitement." Then he smiled that wonderful grin of his that said all is forgiven and you are welcome to come back to my class tomorrow. While being a successful teacher starts with the attitude you bring into the classroom, the real magic often lies in the chemistry generated when you interact with others.

For many years I had my own office which afforded me privacy, solitude and above all space. During my last year, the School needed to reconfigure the Middle School Director's Office, and the space that my office had occupied for many years became victim to the shuffle. With profuse apologies, I was asked if I would mind sharing the rather large area at the back of the Middle School Student Lounge with Mrs. Cheryl Doxas. I knew Cheryl well, for she had been an invaluable asset on my last four British Isles tours, and in particular because of her expertise in looking after the girls. When you are responsible for twenty-six Middle School students 24/7 for fifteen days, you have got to possess a keen sense of humour, and Cheryl was always ready with a smile on her face to step in and take charge in most any circumstance. And her good spirits continued even when we were off the clock. At the end of each day, when our charges were safely down for the night, the teachers would meet for an hour to debrief, relax and consider our plans for the next day. My, how Cheryl constantly made us laugh with her raucous stories and comments, and any stress we were feeling was quickly dissipated by her exuberance.

In London, Cheryl had requested that I take her to a real British pub, and we came across an old Elizabethan-style building which seemed to fit the bill. We entered and Cheryl's eyes lit up at the sight of the bar with its extensive assortment of ales, but it wasn't quite up to snuff.

I took her by the elbow and said, "We're leaving immediately; this isn't a real pub."

"What's wrong with it?", she asked.

"There are no hand-pump ales; this is totally unacceptable!"

My first rule in assessing a good English pub is the quality and number of its cask, or hand-pumped, ales, which are served without the added carbonation that is pumped in when you use more modern draft taps. We went a little farther down the street and discovered a more authentic pub. Little did I know at the time, that before we would leave England, Cheryl would sweet-talk her way behind the bar and try pulling a few hand-pumped ales herself.

I don't think that anyone has ever made me laugh more in my life, as Cheryl always managed to find humour in even the most mundane of situations. We had much in common, and delighted in such interests as history, literature, theatre, music, food, cooking, eating, drinking and even kick-boxing. What a combination! Her major complaint about sharing an office with me came from her husband George, who noted that much of the marking that she used to do at School now seemed to be making its way home with her and he wanted to know why. Cheryl's answer was something to the effect that, because we were constantly kibitzing and having fun, we didn't actually have time to work. "It's impossible to get any work done when Denys is your officemate, George!"

I plead guilty. But even though I too found myself with more "homework", I wouldn't have changed a thing. Our time together, relaxing and enjoying each other's company, recharged our batteries and made us better teachers in our respective classrooms. Rick Barrett was absolutely right when he said, "If you can have fun every day at School with your colleagues … laugh … share a good joke, … and find true friends as I have found, you can have such fun!"

### Teaching is not a Job but a Privilege

Few people get out of bed every morning for thirty-five years and want to go to work. However, I was so very fortunate to discover early in life what I truly wanted to do. My biggest challenge was overcoming my learning difficulties in order to obtain the requisite qualifications and credentials. Even when I gained a measure of success I had to take a different route to get there. Some teachers tolerated and accepted these divergences, while others demanded that I comply with the decreed standards unconditionally. In short, mediocrity masqueraded as compliant good behaviour in some of the classrooms of my day but, my story is not about mediocrity, it is about overcoming it.

I was recently asked what it is that I want my readers to remember most once they've finished reading. The main thing that I hope to have conveyed is that learning is a lifelong journey that is driven by passion. Where there is no enthusiasm, there is no will to learn. Learning doesn't just happen by magic, and I feel confident that my readers now recognize that the acceptance of diversity and hard work are two of the cornerstones of education. Most importantly, I trust I have encouraged my readers to appreciate that the learning experience occurs at the individual level and that the classroom is just the setting or the fertile ground in which this growth occurs.

For each of my thirty-five years of teaching I had a homeroom, and I was often asked if I ever got tired or bored teaching the same grade or subject year after year. My answer was simple: it was, and is, never the same. Every year you have a variety of students with a diversity of strengths and weaknesses, and it is seldom that two students learn exactly the same way. If you believe, as I do, that the individual approach is paramount for each student's success, then every year you are faced with a significant number of new challenges. Each year the students roll-over, and each new class brings with them new possibilities and potential. Finding the answers for all of their peculiar and singular needs is a full-time commitment!

Students learning abilities vary greatly; but there is no one "right" way to learn. What is most important is how that individual learns best. Teachers should always recognize and encourage each student's uniqueness in this regard. For me teaching was not a job but rather a privilege and pleasure, and I enjoyed every minute of my time in a classroom. My students gave a purpose to my life. They kept me young and informed, and I have done my very best to never grow up. Life is so refreshing when seen through the eyes of the most current generation, and I can truthfully say my students have taught me more than I could ever teach them. They were like my sons and daughters.

If I had any success as a teacher, it was due to the fact that I have lived through both success and failure as a student. Indeed, I consider myself somewhat of an expert on failure; I know what it is like to be a failing student at an early age and the effort it takes to emerge successfully from that frustrating beginning. It's all about building success from disadvantage.

A teacher must never forget that students are individual learners first, and only when that is accepted and internalized can they manage the sharing process of this community of learners. As a teacher, I tried to open the lines of communication by always listening to what my students had to say first, for if you listen to them, they might just listen to you in return. Once you have an open dialogue established, you can begin to share your experiences and insights with your class. Students really appreciate honesty and candour and too few teachers are willing to admit their weaknesses to their students. It is by doing so that we become human in their eyes.

Every teacher should remember the wise words of the late Mother Teresa when she said, "We can do no great things, only small things with great love."

# Exeunt

I grew up during the 1950's and 60's, a time which now seems like another world. Although nominally at peace, we lived in the time of the Cold War. Vivid memories of World War II lingered, many of our parents were veterans, and the threat of nuclear war was constant. It was a period of strong family units and small "c" conservatism. Those of us who lived in Montreal knew Big Four Football, and the NHL had not expanded beyond the Original Six. We were told that science would revolutionise the future, but it would be a long time before we saw the nifty technological gadgets of today.

The education system was rule-bound and curriculum-directed, with prerequisites from which you could not opt out. Your typical student had very little choice in what classes they could to take as education came in "streams" of pre-determined courses. Schooling was focused primarily on training a student for the job market. We had to choose where we wanted to go and then we had to plot our path. Changes in methodology were infrequent and there was little use of technology. Education was a means to an end, not a journey of discovery.

While Lower Canada College is an integral part of my story, I hope that I have been able to convey experiences that might have happened at any school. My goal was to recount a more universal story, one that will strike a chord with many whether they went to LCC or not. What I have written is true to the best of my knowledge and memory. I wrote it to be entertaining, but also hope that school administrators, prospective teachers, and students will generally find something of value in what I have written.

My aim is also to give some solace and encouragement to those of you who have an excellent mind but suffer from learning disabilities. I have struggled with such learning difficulties throughout my student life, but despite my problems I became an honours student at university. If I can make it, surely, with the much improved support systems in place today, anyone can as well!

Over the years, I have been fortunate to have had the opportunity to attend many LCC Alumni events, and in conversations with so many alumni, one theme constantly emerges: that some encouragement, advice or suggestion had a much more lasting impact than I could ever have imagined. Many former students have told me that a suggestion or hint that I offered to them at recess, at the lunch table, after a report consultation, or in response to their questions, had, in many cases, a lifelong after-effect. The constructive power that a teacher possesses is quite simply enormous. We may forget once our advice or suggestion is given, but our students don't!

Perhaps my greatest joy in teaching at LCC has been to witness the love and loyalty that so many alumni have for the School. Most students, when they've grown up and gone on to higher education, end up having strong bonds with their universities. Not many students regard their elementary, middle or high schools as the institutions of learning that made the difference in their lives. That is where LCC is so different, because it has the endorsement of such a large group of alumni who have pledged their allegiance and made a lifelong commitment to their old School.

My story of LCC from 1955 to 2005 is for the most part anecdotal – a recollection as both a student and as a teacher. My tenure there coincides with several key events in the history of the School, such as the shift to coeducation, and there were certainly many individuals who have had a lasting effect on me. However, while I am a history teacher, this is not a history book. I chose to share my personal experiences and not attempt to pick up where Dr. Stephen Penton left off in his history of the School, *Non Nobis Solum*. Whereas Dr. Penton made every effort in his book to name and include as many events, students and faculty as possible, I have been selective. I have included the names of a few of my school peers and staff both past and present, but I have purposely not included a single name of any student that I have taught. Certainly there are those whose contributions to the School would receive an honoured place, if not a whole chapter, in this book had I been writing a history; but as they were not integral to the story I was trying to tell, they have not received a mention.

I would be remiss however if I did not single out one individual who shares my passion for history, LCC's sixth Headmaster, Dr. Paul W. Bennett. Paul is a noted author of numerous Canadian historical publications and a man deeply involved with *Historica*. Quite simply, the man lives and breathes history. During his years as Headmaster at LCC, he would always undertake the role of Dr. History during History Night, in a scene called "Dr. History and His Famous Mystery Guests" which was a parody of the classic CBC-TV program *Front Page Challenge*. Paul was always willing (and eager) to make himself available, and his zest, humour and encyclopaedic knowledge made him a quintessential moderator, enhancing every History Night in which he took part. His love for history helped to bring to life that seemingly magical evening each year.

Finally, I am most grateful for the help and support I have received along the way to make this work come to fruition. As my good friend and colleague of many years, Ron Patterson has expressed it, "it takes a village to raise a child and a city of editors to give birth to a book". Without question, I am deeply indebted for the time and effort, and painstaking care that has been given so freely. Richard Andrews, A. Victor Badian, Paul Keyton, Jane Martin, Ron Patterson, and Geoffrey Southwood all tirelessly worked through various drafts and helped brainstorm ideas. Without their encouragement, insight and suggestions, my book might never have been finished. And certainly, without the work of LCC Archivist Jane Martin this book would not have been so aptly illustrated! Many thanks to Jane for her tireless work hunting down just the right photographs to complement my text.

What Ian Griffiths did to assist me in creating and producing twenty-nine History Nights is simply staggering. I could never have developed my program to the level it achieved without his enthusiasm and expertise. His help was simply invaluable: He read various drafts and offered meaningful improvements, but his drawing for the book cover created the tone for what was written therein.

To Peter Johnston (*Negotiating with Giants*) and my wife Lyn Heward (*The Spark: Igniting the Creative Fire That Lives Within Us All*), two highly respected authors in their own right, I thank them for sharing with me their experiences of revising, editing and polishing their manuscripts. Their keen insights and understanding of the writing and publishing process were inestimable. I cannot thank my wife enough for strengthening my sentence structure and transforming my rudimentary vocabulary into a more eloquent prose.

A special thanks goes out to my jury of readers: Kris Alladin, Chris Auclair, Cheryl Doxas, Ingrid Ferrer, Kelly Heward, Jack Hughes, Tariq Jeeroburkhan, Bruce Jenkins, Kirk Llano, Alexandra Mazzella, Gary Millward, Ron Perowne, Maida Rivest, Chris Shannon, Trevor Smith, Jane Slessor, André Trudel and Dave Wood, who read various drafts and offered constructive suggestions and encouragement.

I had a tremendous amount of help along the way refining all the necessary pieces, but I still needed assistance when it came time to put it all together. For that I am beholden to my caring literary editor, Siobhán Quinn, whose guidance transformed my manuscript from a selection of musings into an actual book. I have never claimed to be a professional writer, and so her keen insights and understanding of the writing process were invaluable to the completion of this project.

It would seem that throughout my life I often took the road less travelled, and upon retirement I felt that I had a story to tell that would both amuse and enlighten my readers. I just never realized how difficult it would be to tell "a simple story" and I raise my glass and toast my magnificent "city of editors" that made it all happen.

# References

Barrett, Richard. Conference Address. Teachers' Conference, McGill University Faculty of Education, October 22, 1993.

Biography of Alfred Nobel. Biography.com Encyclopaedia Britannica, 2008. http://www.biography.com/articles/Alfred-Bernhard-Nobel-9424195.

Branson, Richard. Interview. "Richard Branson: Life at 30,000 Feet." By Chris Anderson. TED.com. March 2007. http://www.ted.com/index.php/talks/richard_branson_s_life_at_30_000_feet.html.

Cronkite, Walter. *A Reporter's Life: Walter Cronkite.* New York: Knopf, 1996.

Lickona, Thomas. *Educating Character.* New York; Toronto; London: Bantam Books, 1992.

Penton, D.Stephen. *Non Nobis Solum: The History of Lower Canada College and its Predecessor St. John's School.* Montreal, QC: The Corporation of Lower Canada College, 1972. Printed and bound in Canada by T.H. Best Printing Company Limited, Don Mills, Ontario.

Robinson, Ken. Conference Presentation. "Do Schools Kills Creativity?" TED2006: February 21-26, 2006, Long Beach, California. http:// www.ted.com/index.php/talks/view/id/66RE: TED/TALKS/